Locked Down

A Lesbian Life in Prison

by Idella Serna

The story of Mary (Lee) Dortch

New Victoria Publishers Inc.

Published by New Victoria Publishers, Inc. P.O. Box 27, Norwich, Vermont 05055, a feminist literary and cultural organization.

Cover design Ginger Brown from a drawing by M. Karen Barnes

The original title of this book was Wickets, the small door in a prison door through which food, etc. is passed.

Printed on recycled paper
ISBN 0-934678-40-5

Library of Congress Cataloging-in-Publication Data

Serna, Idella, 1950-
    Locked down : a lesbian in prison / by Idella Serna.
        p.   cm.
    ISBN 0-934678-40-5   :$8.95
    1. Dortch, Mary. 2. women prisoners--Tennessee--Biography.
3. Lesbian--Tennessee--Biography.   I. Title.
HV9468 . S37   1992
365' .43'092--dc20
(B)   92-35499
                                 CIP

In Februrary of 1991, two women from the Arkansas Women's Project, at the request of the publisher, went to visit Lee Dortch and the author (Idella Serna) at the Tennessee Women's Prison in Nashville. Here are some of Dudley's impressions of that visit. (Kerry's observations are included in her foreword to this book).

Dear Beth and Claudia,

I really must admit I truly enjoyed going to Nashville to meet Lee and Lucy. It turned out not to be in the least scary, the place looked like a college dorm (except for the razor wire along the fence!) and the visiting area looked like any bus or plane terminal. We were allowed a private room to talk in so we didn't have an opportunity to see much of any other prisoners.

Lee was a lot less butch looking than I expected—she's put on quite a bit of weight in the last ten years so she has very much a woman's body now, not the thin boyish one of her youth. Her hair is greying, cut short, but with a long tail behind.

The picture of her included in all the papers she gave me does have her looking pretty tough. Her facial hair is quite ordinary—both Kerry and I expected a full beard from the newspaper account and fuss the prison made.

Lucy was quite delightful—smaller than Lee (who's probably five foot eight, but heavy too). She's forty-one, has sparkly blue eyes and grey hair and a sweet face. She's very animated and always touching Lee and looking at her—not in a particularly sexual way, but more just affectionately.

The two of them talked almost non-stop, especially the first half hour we were there (we stayed about five hours in all), often both at once. This was Lee's first visitor in twelve years! Hard to imagine all that time seeing no one from the free world.

Since this was the first time in the history of the Tennessee Women's Prison that visitors were allowed to see two unrelated inmates, we had a picture taken for the prison newspaper. Both Lee and Lucy are terribly excited about the book and are quite the prison celebrities because of it.

Dudley

Foreword

Because of my work with women in prison in Arkansas, I was asked by the publishers of this book to meet with Lee Dortch and the author, in the spring of 1991 at the Tennessee Department of Corrections just outside of Nashville.

In Lee I met a woman who had spent nearly all of her life in prison, a woman excited about the prospect of parole, and a woman whose 29 years of incarceration had left her ill-prepared for the challenges of the free world.

As a young woman, Mary "Lee" Dortch grew up in Russellville, Arkansas. The Russellville of today is a quiet town off the Inter-state, known for its beautiful lake and the nuclear power plant that feeds off the lake's waters. It is like thousands of small towns across the country where the choices for America's sons and daughters are fairly limited. There are few places for employment, everybody knows your business, girls know they will marry boys, and the best and brightest are forced to move away to the big cities.

Lee came of age at a time when there was little support for women who didn't fit society's gender norms. Lee was like count-less women of her time who emulated young rebels like James Dean and Elvis Presley—arrogant, sexual, and defiant. Women who eased the pain of being different through the numbing effects of alcohol. Women who without role models devised ways to get the attention of women to whom they were attracted. Women for whom clandestine bars and clubs provided the only safety for young butches and femmes.

This is the story of the days before the movement for gay and lesbian liberation, when the Mattachine Society and Daughters of Bilitis were making their first tentative starts in San Francisco. It takes place in the days before homosexuality was removed from the list of mental disorders by the American Psychiatric Association and when the medical community had routinely used appalling drug and medical treatments on gay men and lesbians.

Lee's story personifies the history of women in correctional settings over three decades. A story which began in the days before the nation's prisons and jails were jammed with over one million men and women and before 3.2 million people in America were under some kind of correctional control including probation and parole. Before the days when courageous prisoners and their attorneys challenged many cruel and outrageous practices directed at prisoners—challenges which today have placed entire prison systems in 10 states and major institutions in 30 states under court orders to improve prison conditions. It is a story of a prison system that has historically sought punishment and retribution for criminals, not rehabilitation—a story that began when there were few women prisoners, that continues through this last decade in which crime rates stayed essentially stable, though the number of women in prison tripled.

Lee makes no apologies for the life she has led. Faced initially with incarceration for crossing state lines in a car reported stolen by the husband of her lover, Lee went down for the crime in exchange for her girlfriend going free. What followed were a series of attempted prison escapes as a way to free other women or get their attention, murders of people who had mistaken her for a man, and hostage holding of prison officials and physical attacks on other prisoners in an effort to call attention to grievances. Throughout much of this ordeal Lee was being subjected to forced medication in large doses, some of it experimental, to control her behavior.

Lee's story is a plea for help and understanding for herself and for other women like her. Prisoners face many injustices—assignments to a prison far from family or children; job assignment or living segregation based on perceived lesbian identity or HIV infection; lack of job training opportunities or access only to stereotypically female job training in preparation for low-wage jobs; overcrowded and cramped living conditions; inadequate mental health services and psychosocial support; physical threats or brutality by prison staff; little pre-release planning; and few opportunities for post release support.

For too long, society has created an artificial distance between those in prison and those in the free world. Every one of us starts out in a community, in some kind of family, and each of us sets down a road filled with many experiences. For many of us there are serious obstacles—physical violence or the threat of violence by strangers or loved ones, discrimination and hatred based on our gender, race, sexual identity, religion, or physical ability, and society's rigid rules and social mores.

As our prison system explodes, we must come to recognize that locking away those that do not easily fit into society is not a solution. As the Right Wing draws the circle of what is acceptable and what is not even tighter, there will be even more of us who won't fit in. Lee's story is one woman's way of dealing with not fitting in. Can any one of us say what we would do if we found ourselves in her situation?

—*Kerry Lobel*
Lead Organizer, Women in Prison Project
for The Women's Project, Little Rock , Arkansas

CHAPTER 1

"Lee Dortch, 69777, report to the counselor in your dorm," the familiar voice of Officer Deak blared over the prison's loud speakers.

I stood up from filling the brown bag with the commissary purchases for inmate #117005 and wiped the sweat from my forehead. A wave of fear, mixed with excitement, washed over me. After twenty-nine years in prison you have a sixth sense about why you are being called somewhere. I must have been on the docket for parole and the counselor was calling me to discuss my parole plan.

A tight knot gripped my stomach. What kind of parole plan could I give them after twenty-nine years of being isolated from society? I didn't know anyone on the outside anymore. What would it be like? What would it feel like to wear clothes that you pick out for yourself—something different than blue work shirts with Tennessee Department of Correction stamped on the back and jeans with a white strip down the leg. Would I still remember how to drive a car? How did pizza or ice cream taste now?

"Well, I guess you are on this month's docket," Sherron Cooper, my supervisor smiled. "Good Luck."

"Thanks" I smiled back and set the completed commissary order on the counter to be picked up by the inmate later in the day.

Ms. Cooper handed me the pass I would need to get to the dorm during work hours.

As I walked across the yard in the direction of my dorm, a kaleidoscope of thoughts began to spin around in my head. I squeezed my eyes tightly shut to prevent the tears from spilling out in betrayal—tears of joy for my near freedom but also tears for my lost youth, tears for the child that was never accepted by society, the confused child, confused about being homosexual in a society not

1

ready for homosexuality, a society that still thought of homosexuality as a deviant mental illness. When had the confusion stopped and the insanity begun?

Would society accept me now? Had it changed so much in twenty-nine years or would I still be considered the crazy queer? Would I be able to live without the massive dosages of prescribed medications supposed to help me "act normal"—the medication that I knew drove me crazy in the first place. Now I wondered if I had been insane before the drug experiments in the federal mental institution in the 60s, or had the massive dosages of different medication contributed to my insanity? No, I wasn't crazy then, I sighed—not at first. The insanity came after the medication. But who was I to say?

I reached the dorm and my hand froze on the handle of the glass door. My reflection looked back at me. In past years I have never liked to look at myself. I had always worn loose, sloppy clothes to hide my masculine build. I looked at myself now in acceptance.

I looked at my square build, my arms and legs thick and muscular. I looked at all the scars on my arms. The damaged skin was weak and hung loose like a turkey's neck. The rows of scars from razor cuts on top of razor cuts added to the turkey-neck appearance. I usually wore long-sleeved shirts to hide the mutilation but it was too hot today.

Once a child visiting his mother at the prison asked me what had happened to my arms. I hadn't wanted to frighten him so I said that I had been in a car wreck. After that, I made a point of wearing long sleeved shirts on the weekends when kids were visiting, no matter how hot it was.

My hands were not the slim hands of a woman but more like small men's hands, my facial features more masculine than feminine, as well. My hair was my most outstanding characteristic—thick and naturally curly. It was dark when I was a child but had grown silver. I have been told many times how attractive it is—not pretty, but attractive, as you would tell a man how nice his hair looks. My forehead seemed wider and my eyebrows thick, closer to my eyes than a woman's usually were. The facial bones also gave

2

me a masculine appearance. Chin whiskers that grew in abundance completed the masculine picture.

I looked at my eyes—"killer eyes" they have been called in the past. Anger and violence have been in them. But now there was no anger or violence reflected in the glass of the door. Now, I could look back at my reflection and feel secure in seeing me—Mary Catherine (Lee) Dortch, not the frightened kid going from sexual relationship to sexual relationship, not the confused adult, unaware of her role in society—unsure of her gender. Not the emotional mess of twenty-nine years ago but a secure person who realizes that she is not a freak.

I pushed open the glass door to the dorm lobby and showed the guard on duty my pass. He smiled at me knowingly. "Well I guess your time is getting short."

"Yeah, it's downhill all the way." I answered.

I walked to the counselor's office. Her door was open and no one else was in her office. She saw me arrive and motioned me to come in and sit down.

"Well, Lee, I guess you know why I have called for you today, don't you?" She shuffled through a stack of papers on her desk.

I looked at the thick institutional file and nodded. I knew it was about time for me to meet the parole board. "I guess that you are ready for my parole plans."

She picked up several papers from the file and glanced over them. "You have made a considerable improvement in the last two years. You have completed several educational programs and your behavior has done a complete turn around—no write up in over two years. I need to discuss some of your background and family history before we go into your parole plans. Would you care to answer some of my questions?"

My first instinct was to close up—to refuse to answer any questions. I knew what the questions were. It was hard to suddenly begin to tell something that you have spent your whole life keeping a secret; hard to finally reveal your deepest, darkest secrets—the secret that you are more attracted to other women than men and that any relationship with a man feels abnormal—secrets about your hatred toward men—that they only make you feel dirty and

3

used. I found it hard to quit feeling guilty for not being 'normal', to quit feeling unworthy of love. So much had happened.

I tried to recall my past—recall what mattered. I remembered a pretty little town, right in the middle of Arkansas. I wanted to remember the nice things but the nice things had not driven me crazy. Sometimes no matter how we want things to be what we would like, they are not.

My father was thirty years older than my mother and had grown sons by a previous marriage. He adored my mother and they doted on their first born, Sallyann. Sallyann was five years older than I was. My mother died eleven days after my birth. My father was too distraught to continue with the raising of children and felt that girl children would be best raised by a female. He shuffled the responsibility to his widowed sister who had already raised five daughters and two sons.

One of the few memories I have of my father was that he was a man who seldom spoke. He visited us rarely but provided for us financially by having his retirement pension from the railroad sent to his sister.

Sallyann was a quiet child, not unlike our father. She was well-mannered and ladylike. I look back at it all now and wonder if Sallyann's quietness wasn't a buffer for the hurt she was feeling. She had been the only child of doting parents until I was born. She had lost both parents as a result of my birth. The new-born baby demanded most of the attention and Sallyann's hurts were ignored. I wonder now if she didn't withdraw into herself for protection. I always felt that she hated me. We fought constantly as we were growing up.

"Mama took one look at you and died," Sallyann would taunt me. I always felt guilty for the death of this woman Sallyann called mama that I did not know.

Mama—I only knew my aunt as Mama—quit work to assume the responsibility of raising Sallyann and me. Ruby, who was Mama's youngest daughter, still lived at home and helped with our care.

I was a live wire. Mama administered very little discipline and I never liked the word "no." I learned early that if I worried her

4

enough or if I picked her instructions apart—only paid attention to the parts that suited me—I could get my way.

Ruby would shake her head and give a sigh of resignation over Mama's lack of discipline and my willfulness. She would mumble her thoughts under her breath and did much exasperated sighing and rolling of the eyes but never interfered with Mama's wishes.

We lived in an older house near the Arkansas River, the same house where Mama had raised her own children—a clapboard house with a large wooden porch. It had three bedrooms—for Sallyann, Ruby, and Mama—and an upstairs attic room that I used as a bedroom. I could lie in my bed at night and hear the fog-horns of the barges that traveled up and down the river. During the day I liked to run to the river and wave to the ship's captain and crew as they passed. At those times I would feel like Tom Sawyer.

Ruby wasn't as thrilled with the river as I was. She hated the smell of mud and rotting wood caused by living so close. For years, she begged Mama to move to a nicer neighborhood but Mama was set in her ways and was reluctant to leave her home. The condition of the neighborhood wasn't the greatest of Ruby's worries. Her main concern was the annual flooding of the river that ran along the deteriorating houses.

One summer when I was eight, the waters from the swollen river rushed down the street, and were rising to knee level in the house. I watched as Ruby's little poodle swam across the living room to the safety of Ruby's arms. She set him on the closet shelf, safe from the rising water, while she frantically stacked furniture to protect the favorite or more valuable pieces.

I danced a jig in excitement at the rising water, eager for a swim. My cue came when Mama glanced worriedly across the street at an elderly friend. "We'll have to check on Mrs. Hankins as soon as we can," she sighed.

This was all I needed to hear. I dove off the porch—well, more like jumped off the porch—into the raging water. I had not counted on the swift current and was soon pulled under. Each time my head emerged, I could see Mama on the front porch wringing her hands. A cartoon flashed to my mind—a mother hen had hatched a duck's egg, when the duckling followed its natural instinct to take

5

to the water the mother hen would cackle helplessly on the shores.

After I had bobbed under several times and was about to go under again, I felt the firm grip of a man's hand reaching out to me in the water. I heard him call to my Mama. "Relax, Mrs. Rone, I have her."

I had been saved by a neighbor who was caught in the flash flood and had been clinging to a clothesline pole for safety. The two of us maneuvered our way to the nearest front porch and were later transported to our homes by a small rescue boat.

Mama was so relieved that I wasn't hurt she only rebuked me mildly, reminding me that she had forbidden me several times to leave the house and that I had disobeyed her. I assured her with wide-eyed innocence that I thought she wanted me to check on Mrs. Hankins.

Ruby rolled her eyes in exasperation but she wasn't above capitalizing on the situation herself. "Now, I guess you will agree to move. The next flood we have you might not be quite so lucky. Mary Catherine could have died out there," Ruby reminded Mama.

Mama agreed and Ruby found a house in a safer neighborhood.

I had very few friends as a child. I played too rough for the girls and the boys didn't like playing with a little girl. After we moved I met a neighbor boy, David, and we became very good friends. David was a quiet, well-mannered boy who admired my antics.

For as long as I can remember, I have always been prone to melodramatics—if I had a cold it was sure to be fatal, if I found a shiny stone it was sure to be a valuable gem. The first summer of our friendship we were together constantly. David was at my house the day Ruby had sprayed for bugs and spiders, unaware of the cat who was asleep behind the sofa.

When Mama found the cat, she assumed it was dead and laid its body on the back porch for Floyd, her youngest son, to bury.

David, Sallyann, and I gathered around the poor departed cat to pay our last respects. I was immediately struck by "the calling" and decided to pray for the dead cat's eternal soul.

I instructed Sallyann and David to sit in a circle around the dead cat while I laid my hand on the cat's forehead. I prayed like a faith healer I had seen on television. I mimicked the loud shouts of the evangelist's prayers and asked for one of the cat's other eight lives to kick in.

The cat, having had several minutes of fresh air now, was revived from the coma we thought was death by my loud bellow and my hand over his eyes. It sprang off the porch, running across the yard in a panic. The three of us watched, wide-eyed, and our mouths gaped open speechlessly while the cat vomited up his last meal and went about his way.

I was convinced I had the calling. For the rest of the summer, I went about healing everything from Mama's geraniums to the crippled man that sat gossiping on the bench at the courthouse every Saturday.

David and I visited a tent revival. Afterwards, I came home with the announcement that I was saved—from what I didn't know—but the minister told me that if I became saved I would have the world in my hands.

Ruby was getting sick and tired of all this faith healing garbage and felt that the world was not ready to be in the hands of an eight year old. "Oh hush up, Mary Catherine. You don't even know what saved means, besides women can't be preachers."

I thought about this piece of information for a moment and announced. "Well, I'll marry a preacher, then."

David was eager to help me with my cause. "I'm going to be a preacher," he announced.

"Shut up, you ain't neither," I ordered.

Ruby just rolled her eyes and sighed.

I soon abandoned my plans to be a faith healer. If it required marrying David then it lost its appeal. School opened a few weeks after and I started the fourth grade at my new school. I really didn't like school and was bored with the studies.

It was on one of the evenings that Mama was to attend the PTA meeting and Ruby had to work that I learned to distrust men. Mama had asked Floyd to watch me while she went to the meeting.

I enjoyed it when Floyd visited. He was funny and loved to horse-play with me. After an evening of rough playing, I bathed and got ready for bed, laying my school clothes out for the next day. I was stretched out between the cool clean sheets when Floyd came in to tell me good-night. He sat on the edge of the bed. I began to feel frightened and confused when his hand began to rub me under my clothes. When he moved his face near mine, I could smell whiskey on his breath. His whiskers burned my face as he rubbed his cheek against mine. I wanted to cry but I was afraid to say anything. He soon left and I rolled over and covered up my head. When I heard Mama return, I wanted to run out to her but I felt ashamed. What would Mama think of me?

Mama always told me "Big girls don't cry"...I never have done a lot of crying—at least not when anyone could see.

I never liked Floyd after that. I never told anyone but one day I overheard Mama and Ruby discussing an argument between Floyd and his brother, Thurman. Thurman had accused Floyd of putting his hands on his wife. Ruby couldn't believe it and was convinced that the young woman had made it up.

"I don't think she made it up," I added. Mama and Ruby both looked at me in astonishment and I hurried from the room. Nothing was ever said to me about my strange statement but I was never allowed to go anywhere alone with Floyd again.

The summer I was eleven, Ruby began dating an American Indian named Sewell. Ruby never knew what a sadistic man he was. He would make me run and then shoot me with a B-B gun or chase me and twist my arms behind my back when he caught me.

He told me he would kill me if I told Ruby and that she wouldn't believe me even if I did tell.

"If you don't believe me, watch," he said as he took one of my little kittens that I had been watching crawl around in their box, and bashed its head against a tree. I watched in horror as the kitten twitched in pain for a few minutes before dying.

"Did you like that?" he smiled sadistically. "How's about a replay?" He snarled and picked up another kitten. This time it took longer for the kitten to die. It twitched and cried for what seemed like an hour but was only a few minutes. I wanted it to hurry up and die so that it would quit hurting. When the second kitten finally died, he reached for the third and last kitten.

"No, please don't" I begged. "Please...they are just babies," I begged and grabbed up my last little kitten.

8

"Yeah, like you" Sewell laughed.

I froze. Would I be next? He grabbed the third kitten from my arms and smacked it against the tree. It was going to take a long time to die like the last kitten had. I couldn't let it suffer that way. I ran to the kitten and picked it up and smashed it against the tree again, harder. The kitten was quiet. Its suffering had ended. I held the dead kitten in my arms.

Mama and Ruby came out on the porch at that instant. Mama was horrified and screamed.

"What are you doing?"

"It wasn't me...." I started to explain but a warning look from Sewell froze the words in my throat.

"She's had some kind of fit, Mrs. Rone. Just up and killed all her kittens."

I grabbed my dead little kittens and crawled under the porch away from the look of horror on Mama's face. I heard Mama calling to me, but I heard Sewell say, "Leave her there. She will come out when she thinks you won't spank her for killing those cats."

I knew my Mama wouldn't spank me...but she went back in the house. I laid my head down and cried for my beautiful little kittens and for what I was afraid my Mama believed about me. I wondered why Sewell was so mean. I stayed there until it was dark...then I came out.

As long as I can remember, I have been afraid of what was in the dark. If I had to go out in the dark, I would run as fast as I could to get to where I was going. Mama said it was silly. Silly or not, I was afraid but I buried my poor little kittens.

Sometimes Sewell would give me sips of wine or whiskey. I loved the taste and craved the mellow feeling the alcohol gave me.

One hot summer afternoon, the summer I was twelve, I stopped at the service station to have my bicycle tire pumped up.

Mr. McWaters, the owner of Russellville's only service station, was unusually helpful. When my tire was all pumped up, he offered me an ice cold coke to cool me off. Then he invited me to drink it at the back of the garage where it was shady and cool. I accepted his offer gratefully.

It was not until we were in the garage that I began to feel

9

uncomfortable about the offer. Mr. McWaters began to rub his hands over my shoulders and his voice took on a strange quality— quiet and soothing, almost hypnotic. He was standing too close and his breathing became faster. I didn't like his hands on me but I didn't know what to do about it. He had been so nice to buy me a coke and invite me in out of the hot sun. I listened as his hypnotic words droned on, trying to think of a polite way to make my exit.

"You are getting so brown this summer, just like a little ginger-bread cookie," he cooed, rubbing his hands over my sleeveless arm. "I bet you taste as good as a little gingerbread cookie," he said as he tried to kiss me.

I pushed away and tried to focus on his words. He was offering me money to come back later—after the service station closed.

He began to pull crisp bills from his pocket and thrust them into my hand. All I had to do was not tell anyone I was coming back.

I had no intention of coming back but I stuffed the money in the pocket of my jean shorts. Quickly putting the drink bottle in the rack for empties, I hurried back out into the bright light, and grabbed my bike.

I peddled as fast as I could—no destination in mind. When I thought about what had happened I stopped and pulled the money from my pocket and examined it. If Mama saw all this money she would find out that I did something wrong. I was scared. I had to spend the money fast before Mama found out.

I rode my bicycle to the grocery store and spent every penny of the money on candy so that Mama would never find out. I had hoped the candy would make me happy, make the feeling that I was dirty go away, but it didn't.

Three days later, I cursed the leaky patch on my bicycle tire. The air had escaped and I would have to return to the service station for more air.

I pushed my bike in and began pumping the air myself. Maybe I could be through and gone before Mr. McWaters walked out of the garage. But I wasn't fast enough.

"There's my little gingerbread cookie" he called. "Where were you the other night? I thought we had a deal."

Shame washed over me. Mr. McWaters had given me money to

return and I had not. I had cheated an adult.

"Uh...I couldn't. Mama wouldn't let me out of the house unless I told her how I got so much money," I lied.

I noticed the panic that filled Mr. McWaters's face. "You didn't tell her, did you?" he asked in a coarse whisper.

"No, I was afraid she would get mad. I told her I found it." I continued with my lie, my head bowed so that I wouldn't have to look him in the face.

"Good girl, good girl. Here...here take another couple of dollars," he said and thrust two more bills into my hand.

I looked at the two dollars he had just given me and wanted to creep inside myself.

I mumbled a "thank you," as I mounted my bike and peddled away from the service station, my legs heavy with shame. I rode to the grocery store again and quickly spent the money on candy to disperse my shame.

Several times that summer, Mr. McWaters continued to pay me to let him put his hands on my body. He later wanted to put his hands under my clothes like Floyd had done and sometimes he liked to kiss my body under my clothes—calling me his ginger-bread cookie.

I carried the shame of letting him do these foul deeds, but was powerless to stop him. I was afraid he would tell Mama that I had taken his money and spent it. I was afraid Mama would find out and hate me for being bad. I always spent the money quickly because I was worried that Mama would know just as soon as she saw it.

When summer ended and the weather became too cold to ride my bike I had an excuse not to return to the service station. I felt safe that my secret would never be found out.

The traumatic experiences with this man and Floyd and Sewell caused me to be uncomfortable with most men. On the other hand, I was so adored by my Mama and Ruby that I developed an arrogant air about me where most women were concerned.

I was bashful in school and would shrink from friendship with other children. I had few friends at school and did very little visiting around the neighborhood. At school I had little confidence in

11

myself but I was spoiled and willful at home and demanded my way at all times. The lack of discipline and conflicts in my environment at home and school was confusing.

Ruby was my best friend and I loved to make her laugh. I remember when I was fifteen, I found pieces of a mannequin thrown out by a local department store. I solicited the help of Mama and arranged the mannequin in Ruby's bed to resemble a sleeping stranger.

When Ruby got off work, Mama told her that her friend—she couldn't remember her name—had come to spend the night. She had gotten sleepy and Mama had let her go to bed.

We stifled our giggles as Ruby silently tiptoed to the side of the bed to discover the identity of her sleeping friend. When she discovered the charade, she threatened to kill me—forcing herself not to laugh while Mama and I doubled over in laughter.

Another time that summer, Ruby was worried over a few pounds of extra weight and what she thought was the devastating effect it had on her figure. I would roll around on the porch laughing as Ruby mastered the art of balancing the hula-hoop while it whirled around her shapely hips.

She finally decided her efforts were in vain and we got ready to go to the Right Spot, a tavern we cleaned before it opened. I talked her into walking the six miles to the tavern. I assured her I knew a short cut and the exercise would be better than the hula-hoop.

After several hours of beating our way out of thickets and climbing over gullies, Ruby figured out I didn't know a short cut and we were lost. Making our way to the highway we found a small farm and Ruby called home. We waited impatiently for a long time for Sallyann's arrival.

Finally, Ruby saw her coming down the highway, the radio blaring and Sallyann stopping occasionally to make the car bunny-hop to the beat of the music. Later, when she was confronted with Mama's wrath and grounded for being late and bunny-hopping the car, I smirked mischievously because my shenanigan had been ignored.

I heard Ruby mumble, "I'm going to kill you later." I knew Ruby wasn't going to kill me. I had heard that threat a thousand times before.

In high school, when the girls in my class were discussing how cute the boys were, I was thinking how cute the girls were. I didn't have any of the teenage crushes on boys that were so common among the other girls.

When I began to develop breasts, I was ashamed of them. I would wear big sweaters and blouses to hide them. I refused to wear the bras that Mama bought and chose, instead, to wear tight tee shirts that would bind my breasts.

One day, when I was in the tenth grade, I noticed a red stain in my panties. When I wiped myself with the toilet tissue, more blood appeared. I became frightened—I thought I was going to die. I couldn't bear to tell Mama. I knew how hurt she would be. I rolled up toilet tissue to stop the bleeding and remained silent. In a few days the bleeding stopped so I began to think I wasn't dying after all but in a month when the bleeding appeared my fears of dying returned. I became depressed and withdrawn. I couldn't talk with anyone. I was so scared. Again the bleeding stopped and I relaxed. The third time, I decided I would tell Mama—maybe the doctor could save my life.

I ran to where Mama was in the kitchen and threw myself into her arms and began to sob.

"Mary Catherine, what is it child?" Mama insisted and put her arms around me tightly. I was sobbing so hard I couldn't get the words out but I finally managed to explain that I was dying and about the bleeding.

Mama patted me gently. "No honey, you aren't dying. That just happens when you are old enough to start having babies. You will be all right. You just have to be careful with boys."

Sallyann was sitting at the kitchen table. She began to giggle. I felt silly and stupid. I returned to my room in embarrassment. I hated Sallyann. How did she know and I didn't? Sallyann never appeared to have any of the frustrations or confusions that I always seem to have. Her life was neat and orderly. She had many friends at school. She was little and cute and dressed feminine and immaculate while I felt big and clumsy. I felt silly in dresses and preferred to dress in a masculine way.

13

Mama wouldn't explain any further why I had to be careful with boys. And I was too embarrassed to ask. I had already made a fool of myself when I didn't know the bleeding was normal. I couldn't embarrass myself again by asking how I was supposed to be careful. Mama's words of warning only increased my unease in being around men.

With my periods came acute mood swings. I would get my feelings hurt more easily and spend the evening in my room crying over something someone may have said at school or I thought they were thinking about me. I was ashamed to let Mama see me cry and think I was silly. Other times I would become increasingly nervous or restless and couldn't concentrate on my studies. Sometimes, I would be so depressed because I felt dumb and ugly, that I wouldn't want to get out of bed. At times the depression would be so bad that I didn't want to live. I was afraid I was losing my mind.

I spent many hours alone in my room, playing Ruby's old records. I had them all memorized. Ruby read somewhere that a teenager could go crazy spending so much time in her room listening to records, and she would yell at me from the bottom of the stairs to come out. I would ignore her, turning the music up louder to drown out her shouts. When it was meal time I would fix my plate and return to my room. If I did venture out for anything other than school it was usually to the movie theater.

Ruby had a pass that I was allowed to use whenever I wanted to. I would sit for hours watching a movie over and over. I loved the musicals the best.

David continued to be my best friend through high school. He had turned into a nice looking young man. He had coal black hair and eyes to match. He had hopes of us marrying some day. I loved David but I was never going to marry him.

We spent many hours together. His father owned a crop dusting business and David learned to fly a plane before he learned to drive a car. He would take me flying and buy me Juicy Fruit gum so my ears wouldn't pop while we were in the air. It became a game, I would chew a piece just long enough to get all the sugar out and throw it away for another. I could go through a pack of gum in a few minutes. He would buy me several packs at a time.

14

When he got his drivers license we would drive to the lake for a swim and a picnic. One Saturday night, the summer that I was fifteen, David and I had planned on driving to school for a dance. He was going to meet me at the local cafe and we would have a hamburger and drive to the dance. When he didn't show up, I assumed that he had had to work late for his father and ordered my hamburger. When I was finished eating and he still hadn't showed, I went back home. I didn't worry about it too much because David often got tied up working with his father.

At school Monday, Carrie, a friend of David's looked at me strangely. "What are you doing here?" she exclaimed.

I looked at her as if she had lost all her mental faculties. "I guess passing time until graduation." I retorted.

"But, don't you know about David?" she asked, the alarm ringing in her voice.

"Know what?" I replied. A sense of foreboding rose in me like a flood.

"He was killed Saturday night," she explained quietly.

"No. I didn't know," I said, turning from her.

I made it through the rest of the day in a daze. None of the teachers called on me and no one spoke to me.

Later that night I scanned the newspapers for the article about the accident. David had been killed about seven o'clock in the evening—about the time he was to meet me at the cafe. He had stopped for gas and had purchased five packs of Juicy Fruit gum. The gum had been found scattered on the floor of the car. As he pulled off the parking lot of a corner market, a car had hit him in the side. He was killed instantly.

I went to the funeral. David's body was in the casket but it wasn't the David I knew. The David that I had known had been tanned and healthy with curly black hair that tumbled across his forehead and flashing white teeth. The person in the casket was pale and lifeless. His hair was parted on the wrong side and plastered against his forehead. His lips were drawn tightly across his teeth in an artificial smile.

David's death left a void in my life. I became restless and anxious. I never discussed the pain I felt or the loneliness in my life

15

after he was gone. He had always been there to talk with and now there was no one. Sallyann had married in the summer and had moved across town. We had never been close but her absence added to my loneliness.

CHAPTER 2

After David

Carrie, David's friend from school, was a social class above mine. Her father was a doctor. I had never really known her, but she sensed my loneliness and was concerned for me. She began sitting with me at lunch. I loved the attention she gave me. She was a small girl with soft brown hair that hung to her shoulders. She had blue eyes—the color of cornflowers—and an upturned nose. I found myself looking forward to lunch breaks so we could be together. We didn't share any classes together so lunch was the only time I could see her. I would watch her lips while she talked or laughed and wondered what it would be like to kiss her. When she touched my hand or brushed against me a thrill ran through me.

The feelings frightened me. I remembered hearing Mama and Ruby talk about two of my aunts who had been committed to an insane asylum. I began to wonder if I was going insane because I knew my attraction to women couldn't be normal. Also my mood swings increased. I would become restless and, without warning, I would become tired, anxious, or depressed for no reason. At the time I didn't understand that these changes came before my period; I thought only that I must be going crazy.

Mr. Bowers, a neighbor across the street, was a drinker. On occasion he would give me a beer or a glass of whiskey mixed with coke. I began to love the mellow feeling the alcohol gave me. When I drank I didn't have to be afraid of the strange emotions I was experiencing. I could relax and enjoy the warmth of the alcohol, the feeling of security it gave me...a temporary buffer against the world. I began to spend many hours after school with Mr. Bowers.

17

School was to be out soon. I knew I wouldn't be able to see Carrie all summer. I began plotting how I could kiss her. I wanted so badly for her to feel the same way toward me that I felt toward her.

"Hey, Carrie," I said as she slid into the chair across from me.

"Hi Mary. Boy, am I glad it's Friday. This algebra has warped my brain. I need a break." She laughed.

I pounced on the opportunity, "How about a movie tonight? *Rebel Without a Cause* is playing."

"I know," she breathed, "I think that James Dean is the greatest. I saw it twice last weekend."

"Want 'a see it again," I offered, hopefully.

"Nah, thanks anyway." She smiled. "I have to wash my hair. As thick as it is, it takes all weekend to dry when it's rolled up."

My spirits fell. I guess that pretty much covered the weekend.

I went to the movie Friday by myself. James Dean was really a lady killer. In one scene he took a switch blade from a hood and beat him up. The movie was full of wild car races. The girls all adored him. In the end he died—it was all so sad and romantic. I watched the movie and longed to be adored by Carrie like the girls adored James Dean.

I spent Saturday morning moping around in my room. I couldn't get last night's movie out of my mind. I wanted Carrie to look at me like the girls looked at James Dean. I felt like I too was "A Rebel Without a Cause." I stood in front of the mirror— the collar of my shirt turned up— combing my hair like James Dean.

"Mary," I heard Ruby call me from downstairs. "Want to go to the Right Spot with me this morning?"

I started to say no, but then changed my mind. I enjoyed our after-hours job cleaning the Right Spot. I was a big help to Ruby and went with her on most of the cleaning trips. It gave me a chance to sneak drinks of whiskey—a drink I had grown used to since those sips from Sewell's bottle. I had developed the habit of sneaking whiskey any time I could—from visitors, neighbors, or from The Right Spot. I hurried down the stairs.

We finished the job of cleaning the dance hall quickly and I tucked the bottle of whiskey that the owner kept under the counter beneath my shirt. I also noticed an old revolver lying under the cash register counter. I wanted Carrie to notice me. If I could do something brave and daring I figured I could impress her and she would fall in love with me. The gun was what I needed to impress her. I hadn't decided yet what I intended to do with it, but, without Ruby noticing, I tucked the ancient gun in my belt and hurried to the car.

I spent the rest of the afternoon in my room. I combed my hair a dozen times. With my dark hair and green eyes I imagined that I resembled the young Elvis Presley who was becoming popular. I mixed several glasses of whiskey and coke and drank them.

By nightfall, I still hadn't come up with a plan to impress Carrie. I decided to play it by ear—sure that an opportunity would present itself. I was overly shy, but armed with the courage alcohol gave me, I walked the few miles to Carrie's house. The alcohol didn't give me the courage I needed to approach Carrie, but I held her neighbors, an English teacher at the school, and her husband and child hostage at gun point.

My plan didn't include anything beyond showing Carrie what a bad-ass I could be. After several hours, I began to sober up and my courage began to seep away. I sighed in resignation. I also realized that I had made a fool of myself and that Carrie would probably never have anything to do with me again. Well, I didn't care. I didn't like her anyway. She was a bitchy snob. In fact, I decided, I hated her. I searched my mind for a reason to abandon my hostages suddenly. A reason that wouldn't seem ridiculous—not that what I was doing wasn't ridiculous. Nothing came to mind. I quit searching and said what I really felt. "I'm hungry. I'll see you later," I announced and walked out, leaving my hostages terrified and confused.

"Tell Carrie. I came by to kill her...and I will." I called back in a final effort at proving my masculinity and toughness.

I headed for the local theater.

"That's a mighty fine gun you have there. Where did you get it?" the owner of the theater asked me.

"I stole it from the Right Spot," I answered, still feeling a need to show off, and moved to the refreshment counter to purchase a box of bon-bons.

I had just paid for my candy when the constable called to me. I made a mad dash for the door.

With the speed of youth, I ran to the parking lot of the Kroger store and spotted a man getting into his car. As I jumped in, he jumped out—leaving me with a 'get-away car.'

After a thirty-minute chase by the local sheriff's department, I stopped for gas, waving the pistol in the air and thanking the service-station attendant in a cock-sure manner—much like what I imagined James Dean would do.

The chase ended when four patrol cars caught up with me and cut me off the road. Feeling trapped, I looked around for an escape. Another car had pulled off the road, leaving it clear for the high speed chase. I ran to the car for protection. A mental picture of me dying in a shoot-out and Carrie mourning me flashed through my mind. It was a touching picture.

A woman's terrified screams penetrated the frenzied state of excitement the evening had put me in. "Please don't shoot. I have a child with me," she cried.

"Don't shoot, you may hit her car. I'll throw my gun out," I called to the officers, my voice full of defeat.

The sheriff's deputies surrounded me and snapped the handcuffs on my wrist in a typical arrest. When the officer rubbed his hands down my body to ensure that there were no other weapons he cursed, "My god, it's a damn girl."

I was sent to a state hospital for a thirty day mental evaluation. In those days an identity crisis wasn't considered a mental disorder, nor was there any recognition of hormone imbalances or severe PMS. Either you saw pink elephants or you didn't—there was no in between. I wasn't considered mentally unstable, and was held accountable for my actions. My impulsive behavior was attributed to lack of discipline. My punishment was left to the discretion of the judge.

I stood shame-faced in front of the stern judge. "Well young lady, what do you have to say in defense of your behavior?" he demanded.

"I can't...I won't...just lock me up," I said defiantly.

The judge was prepared to send me to the girl's reformatory

when Ruby spoke up. "Your honor. Mary isn't a bad girl, I'm sure this Carrie girl had to do something to her for Mary to act the way she did."

The judge hesitated but with Ruby's coaxing, he agreed to let me go live with my father. "Perhaps the firm discipline from a man is what she needs," the judge decided.

I was packed up and carted off to my father's house. My father was a tall, stern man of German descent. He was in his seventies and had silver gray hair and dressed in black. He lived by the "Good Book" and preached at a small church on Sundays. What discipline my Mama failed to administer, my father made up for ten-fold.

He expected me in bed when the sun went down and up by dawn to do chores before school. My homework was done first thing after coming home from school and he over-saw its completion. It is normal for all sixteen-year-olds to resent authority. But I think I was more resentful of his authority because of my dislike of men and my discomfort around them.

He didn't approve of my boyish hair cut. "A woman's hair is her crown and glory," he would scold. I resented his criticism and sought an outlet for my resentfulness.

Dansville was a small town. The central points of social life were the two bars or the church. I chose the two bars.

After the first week, I began to slip out the bedroom window and walk the few miles to the local bars. No one worried about serving minors then—if you had the money you were old enough to drink. My father gave me money to use for the school lunches. I chose instead to eat a bag of chips and save the money. Combining the money my father gave me for chores and the money that Ruby and Mama sent me, I had enough to finance my evenings out.

I would sit at a table and drink several beers and listen to the juke box. The bar was owned by a man called Ted. He was married to a fleshy woman, called Mable, who ran the other bar in town.

I began to notice a woman that Mable spent a lot of time with. She was a small woman in her mid-thirties. She wore her dark hair long and her sweaters were tight across her firm breast. Every time I looked in her direction she seemed to be looking at me. Finally,

21

one night I ordered her a beer and had the waitress take it to her. She accepted it and walked across the room to my table.

"Thanks kid, mind if I join you?" she said, indicating the empty chair.

"Go ahead." I answered and pushed the chair with my foot—in a manner I had seen in an Elliott Ness movie. I caught the faint scent of her perfume as she sat down and it caused strange stirrings in me.

"What's your name, kid?" she asked.

"Mary Dortch," I answered.

"Dortch?" she laughed loudly. "The preacher's kid?"

"Yeah, that's me," I answered shyly.

"Well, I bet he would shit if he knew you were here."

"Probably," I agreed, "you going to tell him?"

"Nah, you're too cute to make trouble for. How did you escape the preacher, anyway?" she asked.

"He goes to bed with the chickens—I wait until he's asleep and climb out the window," I explained.

"Well I'm glad to meet you, kid. My name is Minnie."

I smiled and we spent the evening drinking and talking. I ended up at her trailer and in her bed. I returned just before daylight, exhausted but happy.

We spent every night together for the next two weeks. Minnie showed me how to please a woman sexually and was experienced at pleasing. I learned that she and Mable were lovers. Ted, Mable's husband was aware of the relationship but didn't kick up a fuss as long as Mable kept him happy.

Mable wasn't quite as obliging as Ted was. When the rumors of our affair reached her ears she confronted Minnie in the bar one evening. "What the hell is going on?" she demanded.

"None of your damn business," Minnie answered her.

"The hell you say," she shouted and grabbed Minnie by the hair.

I was up and over the table like lightning and knocked Mable to the floor. Powered by the strength of youth and alcohol and the desire to defend "my woman," I pounded my fist into the fleshy face of Mable, again and again.

22

I was suddenly lifted off Mable's chest and flung across the room. A man's fist began to pound my face. Before the first blinding blow I saw Ted. His huge, meaty fist hit me three more times before he tossed me out of the bar, ordering me not to come back until I sobered up.

The next morning, when my father saw my face he was furious. He couldn't imagine what kind of man would beat a girl like I had been beaten. My father assumed that Ted had intended to rape me, so he and my four half-brothers, armed with shotguns, went looking for Ted.

When my father returned, I could tell by the look on his face that Ted had told him about Minnie and me. My father wouldn't look me in the eye. He never said anything to me but called my Mama and told her he was sending me home. I went home in disgrace.

When I arrived home, Mama had to call the judge and let him know that I had not stayed at my father's house. I was sent to the girl's reformatory.

At the girl's reformatory, I was locked in a room by myself for fifteen days of quarantine. The room was dormitory style with a wooden door, and no bars on the window. A wicket in the door was used to pass me food and mail. The door was left open for ventilation and many of the other girls would call to me or send me kites (notes folded in a triangle), telling me what it would be like when I was released into population. There were only thirty girls housed at the institution and I learned many of their names in the first few days.

I was served three meals a day in my cell. The food was good. Much of it was raised by the girls housed at the reformatory. I could see the yard from my window and it spread over several acres of farm land. A waist-high barbed-wire fence surrounded the area. I learned later that the purpose of the fence was to keep the institution's cows out rather than to ensure that the girls stayed in. Barns and sheds, as well as cottages for staff members, were also on the premises.

The institution's nurse visited me regularly. She was a short, plump woman with a Mrs. Santa Claus personality—you couldn't help but like her. She told me the first day of my arrival that everyone called her Mama Dee.

"Well Mary, you will be getting out of isolation today," Mama Dee told me when she made her regular rounds. "We try to house two girls to a room. It has always been our practice to allow the girls a chance to mingle and find a girl that they would like to room with. Some of the girls prefer to room by themselves, but we encourage the girls to have a roomy. It helps to keep you from getting homesick. Why don't you leave your things here until after dinner tonight. That way you'll have a chance to pick out a roomy."

"That sounds great to me. Can I go to the dayroom now?" I asked.

"Sure." Mama Dee opened the door for me to pass through.

I was shy at first about walking into a room of people I didn't know, but I was quickly put at ease. The girls surrounded me with questions and offers to share toiletries or other personal belongings.

At lunch I sat with a girl named Patty. She had long, teased, blond hair that she sprayed stiff. She wore bright red lipstick and nail polish, tight jeans, a pink T-shirt and leather boots. She carried her cigarette pack rolled in the cuff of her T-shirt. The whole effect was a tough girl look.

"Have you picked out a roomy yet?" she asked.

"Nah, Mama Dee said I could wait until after dinner. How about you, do you have a roommate?" "Yeah. I have one but she's a slob...snores all night. I could ask her to move if you want to move in with me."

"Won't she get mad?" I asked, concerned.

"Nah, she don't like rooming with me, she's just been too chicken-shit to ask to move out. She'll be glad I asked her to move."

"Okay, then," I agreed eagerly.

"Good. I'll tell her now and you can move in right after lunch," she said as she stood up. She walked over to a table and I watched her as she talked to a pudgy girl. Then I saw the girl look in my direction and nod in agreement. Patty returned to the table and we finished our meal and went to gather my belongings to move into her room.

The room had two twin-sized beds and two chests of drawers. A writing desk sat at an angle in one of the corners. The beds were covered with blue cord spreads. White cotton curtains trimmed in

24

blue rick-rack hung over the only window. A bed-side lamp and a blue throw-rug added to the dormitory look.

Our days were busy because we were all assigned jobs. I was assigned to work with Mama Dee to clean the clinic, keep the medical records in order and sterilize the equipment. I enjoyed most of the work and I enjoyed working with Mama Dee. I liked the special attention she bestowed on me—little things like extra cigarettes and snacks.

As the nurse's aide, one of my duties was to give the girls a Waserman—a culture smear taken with a wooden spatula—to test for venereal disease. I didn't like this part of my duties. I wanted to protect them from what I considered a forced invasion—instead I was the invader.

Our evenings were free. We could spend them in the rec-room where there was a pool table and a ping-pong table. Or we could read or stay in our rooms.

I was very comfortable with the arrangement with Patty. She had a record player and a large collection of records. We spent a lot of time playing them. She taught me to dance and I loved to slow dance. She felt so good in my arms. At night I began to plot about how I could make love to her.

Sometimes on Friday or Saturday we were allowed to go skating or to the movies in group outings. I always enjoyed these outings. It was almost like a date. One stormy night after returning from seeing a horror movie Patty was too afraid to go asleep. Every time the lightning cracked she would cry out and cover up her head.

"Do you want me to sleep with you?" I asked with pretended innocence.

"God, yes, I can't stand this lightning," she exclaimed.

My spirits rose. This was the chance I had been waiting for. Patty had been sexually promiscuous prior to her incarceration. After I was snuggled in her bed, it was easy to arouse her. I spent the night making love to her. There was no worry of being caught. Once we were in our rooms for the night, the doors were locked and no one came to check on us unless someone called for the nurse.

After that night, Patty and I were accepted as a couple. I was finally able to acknowledge I was homosexual. Having a masculine appearance had it's advantages when housed with thirty sexually deprived young women. I did a lot of flirting and enjoyed the attention I got from suitors. Patty watched me jealously and was quick to fight if she walked into the day-room area and caught me playing pool with another girl or talking with someone when she wasn't around. I would play Elvis Presley records and twist my hips in imitation of him to entertain my female fans. They would squeal with delight. Patty would watch in anger.

The superintendent of the institution thought I was disruptive to the other girls. She would send me on errands and assign me chores other than my regular duties to discourage my influence on the other girls.

Patty wanted to get me away from the other girls. We would talk together at night about escaping. I was willing to go anywhere Patty wanted to go. Patty had plans of going to California to be in the movies. Her plans became my plans.

One evening the local theater had gangster night. They showed news clips of notorious gangsters. Pretty Boy Floyd, Bonnie and Clyde, and Dillinger were among the gangsters that were glamorized. The bullet riddled car that Bonnie and Clyde were eventually killed in was brought to the theater and put on display.

Patty and I returned from the movie theater full of exciting plans—we were going to be the next Bonnie and Clyde team.

We made our plans that night to escape. We would steal and rob our way across the country making it to Hollywood where we would have enough money to live on until we became famous movie stars.

I began stuffing clothes and other belongings into a pillow case, preparing for our escape.

"Hurry Mary," Patty whispered as she raised the window. "Get the knife from under the mattress and let's cut this screen."

I hurried across the room with the butcher knife she had stolen from the kitchen weeks ago when we first began our plans to run away. I slid the blade of the knife around the window facing cutting the screen away enough that we could slip out and drop to

26

the soft ground below.

"Come on, let's run," I whispered and grabbed her hand. We ran across the yard until we reached the barbed-wire fence. I pushed one strain of the fence down with my foot and held the other strain up with my hand, creating a space for Patty to crawl through. She threw her pillowcase full of clothes through the fence and followed it, turning to hold the fence apart for me to crawl through.

I had just started through when someone grabbed me by the collar. I tried to struggle but I was jerked back through the fence and to my feet. Patty squealed out in terror.

Officer Hale, the only male officer on the compound, held me at an arm's length, anger distorting his face. In the dark night he looked like Satan himself. He dragged me back to the dorm. I kicked out and swung my fist wildly but neither hit my mark. Patty picked up our clothes and followed meekly. The night was too dark for her to venture alone.

I was taken to the superintendent's office. She arrived shortly in her bathrobe with a stern look on her face. "Well, Mary Catherine and Patty, what have you two to say for yourselves?"

"It was all my fault," I offered in an effort at keeping Patty from receiving any disciplinary action.

"I have no doubt that the idea originated with you Mary," the superintendent agreed, "but you were both caught running away. I am forced to keep you locked down for thirty days. Those are the rules."

With that, she waved her hand in the direction of Officer Hale and he escorted the two of us to the rooms used for isolation and locked us in.

The next few days in isolation only made us more determined to carry out our plans. I would call to Patty in the next room and we evaluated the situation. We both agreed that Patty should have gone on the night of our escape. If one of us was free then she could come back for the other one. I began to make my plans of escaping without Patty. I would be her hero by coming back and rescuing her.

When the door was open to bring me clean linens, I pushed the door wider and ran through. I ran down the hall and out the front door of the dorm. I could hear the officer on duty calling for assistance. I ran faster, the sound of my footsteps pounding in my ears. But the heavy sound of men's footsteps soon began to drown the sound of my own running feet. I glanced over my shoulder without slowing my pace. Officer Hale was hot on my trail. My heart skipped a beat and my pulse quickened as I tried to increase my speed. I ran down the hill from the institution but he caught up with me near the bottom. He grabbed me by the hair and began to beat me severely around the head and shoulders, kicking me whenever I fell to my knees, then jerking me to my feet by my hair. He dragged me back to the institution and threw me in my cell.

Mama Dee was appalled by my battered face the next day and threatened to contact the governor for my immediate release.

Three days later, Mama and Ruby came to get me. Mama was given a bottle of thorozine upon my release with the instructions to administer it to me to keep me under control. Mama tossed the medication in the garbage. "There isn't anything wrong with Mary Catherine," she said, sniffing.

Because of the incident concerning Carrie and the violent act against the staff member, who was Carrie's neighbor, I could not return to school. The principal explained that because I had been in a reformatory that I was permanently expelled from school. Mama was ignorant of the law and accepted his explanation.

I became bored and increasingly restless just sitting around the house. I tried to contact Patty but all my letters were returned. The institution did not let former residents correspond with inmates. We had been separated so suddenly that I did not get her home address. I knew what town she lived in but I was not successful in finding her address.

After several months of trying to get in touch with her, I was pleasantly surprised to have a visitor from the reformatory. She had worked in the mail room when my letters had been returned and had gotten my address. She was out now. She didn't know where Patty lived but she had remembered that she was planning on going to California.

CHAPTER 3

On my Own

The wheels of my mind began to turn. I began to make plans to travel to California. There I would become rich and find Patty. Jean, the girl from the reformatory was willing to go with me. She was from an abusive home and had no plans of returning to the abuse again.

We pooled our money. If we saved the cost of bus fare by hitch-hiking we figured we could rent a room and live on sandwiches until we got jobs.

That night, after Ruby and Mama had gone to sleep, we slipped out of the house. With our bags of clothes, we walked through the darkness towards the highway. There, we were sure we could catch a ride with a truck driver going in the direction of California. Thirty minutes after we arrived at the truck stop we had a ride.

The truck driver was glad for the company and we told him about our plans on the trip. We both lied about our age, claiming we were over twenty-one. We were able to ride with him most of the three day trip. He dropped us off at another truck stop with good luck wishes, where we were able to get another truck which took us almost to Los Angeles. We walked a short distance and hitched another ride with a truck driver who took us the rest of the way.

We looked up at the road sign that read 'Hollywood' with stars in our eyes.

Our dreams were soon to be dampened. Millions of young people came to Hollywood every year to become movie stars. We didn't know the first thing about trying to make it in the movies.

We found a small room in a run-down section of Los Angeles.

We had to step over winos who lay sprawled on the stairway to make our way to our room. The hall was lighted by a single bare light bulb in the ceiling. The walls were painted dark green which contributed to the gloom. When we unlocked the door to our room, its condition did nothing to lift our spirits. The room had a foul smell of urine, sweat, and tobacco smoke. Faded wall paper was peeling from the walls. A metal double bed covered with a gold spread was in the center of the room. A green plastic chair with sagging springs sat in one corner. A warped dresser with a foggy mirror occupied another corner of the room.

The rent cost us the better part of our grub-stake. We had very little left to buy the sandwiches we had planned to live on until we struck it rich.

"Well this won't be for long. We can find a job to keep us going and we will be rich before we know it," I said as we dumped our clothes on the lumpy mattress.

Neither of us slept well that night. We were both too excited about the prospect of finding a job and then making it big in the movies. We lay awake listening to the drunks cursing each other and the man in the next apartment slapping his wife around because she failed to keep the baby quiet while he slept.

The next morning we both began to search for jobs. After several days of job hunting, I realized I was not trained in anything. My feet hurt from all the walking and I was tired from the lack of sleep the night before. I had just about given up my search when a sign in the window of an x-rated book store caught my eye. "We make movies" the sign read.

My spirits soared. I realized the sign was advertising x-rated movies but I figured that if they made movies of any kind they were bound to know other people who made movies. I began to hope that this was my chance to meet someone in the movie business.

I entered the shop. An overweight woman sat behind the counter on a high stool. She wore a pair of tan stretch-slacks. The rolls of excess fat, molded around the seat of the stool, reminded me of the yeast bread that Mama would set out to let rise. Her hair was a brassy red with black roots and she wore bright green eye shadow over the lid of her eyes, accenting their puffiness.

"Hi, can I fill out an application for a job here?" I asked.

"What makes you think there are any job openings?"

"I am only hoping that there are," I said, putting on my best smile.

The women stared at my face before answering. "You a little butch?"

I was taken back by her bold question but answered honestly. "Yes, is it a problem?"

The women's loud laughter filled the room. "Problem...hell no, it ain't no problem. It's an asset for the job. You over twenty-one?"

Yeah," I lied.

"Sure you are, and I am only twenty-five," she replied, her voice full of skepticism. "Can you work four to twelve?"

My spirits rose. She was going to give me the job—and the night shift would mean that I would have the mornings free for auditions.

"I sure can," I answered eagerly.

"Good, come back at four this evening and I will get you started."

I left the store full of excitement. I had a job...it was a start.

Jean got a job working a gay bar. Jean wasn't gay but the money and tips were okay. I would spend my evenings after work at the bar. My second night at the bar, I met a woman who was eager for my company.

"Hi, sweety," she purred and sat down at my table. The strong scent of her cheap perfume filled my nostrils.

"Hi, I said." She was a slim woman in her mid-forties. Her hair was raven black—so black it had an artificial look to it. It was sprayed stiff and the ends were fussed. Her make-up had been applied in layers. Dark black eyeliner gave her dull eyes a raccoon look.

"Mind if I sit here? You look so lonely," she said.

"No, I don't mind. I'm waiting for my friend to get off work." I nodded my head in Jean's direction across the room.

She looked in that direction. "Well I hope she has a long time before she gets off work." She gave a loud laugh at her own wit and

31

pulled her chair closer to mine.

I didn't wait for Jean that night. Instead, I left the bar with my new companion. I learned that her name was Bonnie—that was all I learned about her. We went to several other bars before ending up at a motel.

In the following weeks, I met several women who were in search of lesbian companionship and would spend the night with them. These women would spend money lavishly on me, and were generous with gifts of money. Sometimes these relationships would last for a week or so—until one of us would become bored—but most of them were only for one night.

Jean got tired of the gay bar and decided to hit the street. "I can get paid for what my old man took from me for free most of my life," she explained to me.

"Don't be a fool. We didn't come out here to be prostitutes." I argued.

"And what do you think that you have been doing since we got here?" she hurled at me, her face full of contempt. "Sleeping with those rich bitches for pay is the same thing as sleeping with men for pay. It's all prostitution, anyway you look at it."

I felt as if she had slapped me in the face. She was right. Suddenly, I felt used and dirty. I wanted to go home.

That night I called Mama. She wired me money to buy a bus ticket back to Russellville.

Ruby and Mama were at the bus station when I arrived home. Mama had lost weight from worrying over me. They had been sure I was dead.

"Where have you been...we have been worried sick...why didn't you call?" Ruby demanded.

Mama hugged me tightly. "Leave her alone. She is back now, and she won't do it anymore."

The restlessness soon returned. In a small town like Russellville my reputation was well known. 'Nice people' didn't want anything to do with me.

I decided to join the Air Force. I rode the bus to Little Rock to the Air Force recruiter's office. The recruiter explained that four years was the minimum to enlist. That was fine with me. But later that evening when I told Ruby and Mama of my plans, Mama cried—four years was a long time to be away from home.

I ignored her tears, determined that the military was what I wanted.

On my next trip to Little Rock where I was to begin my enlistment tests and receive my physical, I remembered that Mama Dee, my supervisor at the girl's reformatory, had mentioned that she lived in Little Rock. During a break in the testing, I found her telephone number in the phone book and called her.

She was pleased to hear from me and invited me over to the house for dinner and to meet her family. I accepted the invitation and later that night I was introduced to Mama Dee's daughter, Joyce and two granddaughters, Carol and Ann.

Joyce's husband was a construction worker who worked out of state. Since Mama Dee stayed at the girl's reformatory most of the time, Joyce had found it was easier for her and her daughters to live with Mama Dee. They felt it was ridiculous to maintain two households when both were only used part time.

They were a warm, close family and after dinner we all played records and took turns dancing with each other. Joyce laughed easily and enjoyed herself as much as a kid. My imitation of Elvis Presley had the same effect on her as it had on the girls at the reformatory. I began a concentrated play for her attention, grabbing chances to dance with her and pulling her close during slow dances.

When it began to grow late, Mama Dee invited me to spend the weekend. I accepted the invitation with the determination to use the weekend to win Joyce's heart.

I tried every manipulation in the book. I was adorable, sweet, sexy, pitiful, and cute—I tried everything. I had the advantage because Joyce wasn't aware of what was happening.

By Sunday evening, I could sense I had won. I could tell that I had stirred something in her, something she wasn't aware existed. I knew that she would be alarmed if she realized that she was attracted to me. My instincts told me that I needed to push forward before she ran like a frightened rabbit.

After everyone had gone to bed, I walked into Joyce's room,

using the pretense that I was frightened. After several minutes of my pitiful pleadings she reluctantly agreed to allow me to sleep with her. I climbed in and snuggled close to her body. She was soon to regret her offer and the next few minutes were spent with Joyce removing my hands from her body, which would quickly move to another part of her body. Her warnings and threats soon began to wear thin and I sensed she was relenting, partly out of curiosity and partly out of desire.

Monday morning, Joyce drove me home only to return the next Friday for me to spend the weekend again. For the next six months we established a pattern of her picking me up on Friday and returning me home on Monday.

Mama and Ruby were not pleased with this new friendship and assumed that a woman near forty that kept the company of a girl of seventeen was up to no good. They both thought that the woman was taking me to bars to use my youth as bait to attract men. I smiled at their innocence.

I decided that Mama was right about four years being too long to be away from home and abandoned my plans to join the air force. I never mentioned to Mama or Ruby that the recruiter had told me that I would be stationed less than one hundred miles from home.

Our weekend routine was interrupted when Joyce's husband returned home unexpectedly. She had already picked me up and I was at her house when her husband arrived. She introduced me to him as Carol and Ann's friend. I spent the weekend in Carol's room playing records and dancing.

Monday morning, Joyce's husband left to go back to his job site. Joyce waved to him from the kitchen door. "Whew, I'm glad this weekend is over," she sighed.

"Me too," I agreed as I poured myself a cup of coffee and sat down at the kitchen table.

"Well, I don't know why," she teased. "You and Carol sounded as if you were having a ball last night,"

"We did," I agreed innocently.

Joyce went into an immediate rage. Her face turned red and she began to scream hysterically. I didn't understand what I had done.

"You bastard!" she screamed. "She is just a kid."

"So am I," I pointed out, still not understanding her anger.

Joyce ran to the bedroom. I sat at the kitchen table, trying to figure out what I had done. I had stayed in Carol's room and even enjoyed the evening. I hadn't given her husband any hint that there was anything between Joyce and me.

When Joyce returned, she was carrying a gun. Her face was still wild with anger. I jumped to my feet. Fear gripped my heart like a giant vise.

"Let's go," she said and indicated the kitchen door by pointing with the gun.

"Honey," I pleaded, "what have I done to make you so angry?"

"Don't play innocent with me," she hissed. "I trusted you...and with my own daughter," she cried.

A light of understanding washed over me. "No Honey, you are wrong. It wasn't like that. We just played records. That's all," I tried to reason with her but she was too wild with anger to listen to reason.

"Move, you bastard," she ordered again.

I obeyed and walked out the back door. Joyce followed close behind.

"Get in the car," she ordered. "You drive."

"Drive where?" I asked.

"Just drive," she screamed.

"Okay, Okay," I agreed, not wanting to upset her any further. I was beginning to realize that Joyce really was planning to kill me.

As I drove, I tried to explain to Joyce that nothing had happened, but she would not hear a thing I said. She continued to hold the gun aimed at my head while her eyes scanned the rural lands we were passing. Finally we came to a thickly wooded area. "Pull over here" she demanded, indicating a wide area in the shoulder of the road. "Now, get out" she commanded after I had pulled the car to a stop.

"Joyce...don't do this," I pleaded. "I swear to you nothing happened."

"Move!" she shouted, still pointing with the gun.

My heart was beating in a wild rhythm. Joyce wasn't playing. I couldn't talk her out of it; she was going to kill me. I continued to plead with her as we walked into the woods, the gun aimed at my back.

My chance came when Joyce stumbled over a root. I turned quickly and wrestled with her for the gun—finally wrenching it from her hands.

She stared into my eyes with icy cold eyes, then turned silently and walked back to the car, leaving me standing with the gun in my hand.

During the next few weeks, I wrote several letters begging her to write me and I tried calling her house several times. She refused to talk with me on the phone and my letters were never answered.

Mama and Ruby were pleased about the break-up. Neither had ever realized that we had been lovers and assumed that Joyce had found her a man and didn't need me as bait anymore.

Mama interpreted my hurt as restlessness and plotted my future with a family acquaintance.

I was working part-time at a hamburger stand close by. Artie Lewis Boyd began to have his lunches at the hamburger stand. He flirted with me occasionally, telling me how cute I was. I ignored his remarks, thinking that those kinds of remarks came with the job.

I was surprised one evening when I came home and discovered Artie Boyd visiting Mama. I glanced into the living room from the hallway before starting up the stairs to my room but Mama's voice stopped me. "Mary, come into the living room. There's someone I want you to meet."

I obeyed. "I have already met Mr. Boyd," I assured her as I went in the living room and parked myself on the arm of her chair.

"Yes, Mary and I met at the hamburger stand where she works. How are you doing, Mary?" he greeted.

"Fine," I answered. "I didn't know you knew my Mama." I was suspicious.

"Yes, Lillie and I have been friends for a very long time. I just stopped by to see if she wanted to go to the movies—you too."

I was still suspicious but it couldn't be too bad if Mama was going with him. "Sounds okay to me." "Good, I'll leave now and give you a chance to get ready. Don't dress up. We'll go to the drive-in. Don't bother with fixing dinner. We'll grab a bite to eat at the snack bar."

Artie left, to return in two hours to take Mama and me to the movies. He was a tall, sturdily built man in his mid-forties. A touch of gray sprinkled his hair. He owned a construction company and was bronze and muscular from working hard labor in the sun. We enjoyed the evening. Artie lavished offers of snacks on me and allowed me to drive his car home. He was a quiet man but had a dry wit about him. I found myself enjoying his company very much.

Over the next few weeks, Artie became a regular visitor. His wife had died over ten years before, and his three sons were all grown, so Mama invited him over for dinner often. He took us out just as often. We would go to the movies or shopping. Artie seemed to enjoy spending money on me—buying me many presents. I was at an age when a kid loves a car and he would encourage me to use his car frequently.

We developed a warm friendship. I never suspected that Artie was falling in love with me, so I didn't see it coming when he announced that he had approached Mama with his request for my hand in marriage. We were sitting in the living room when he made the announcement. I was speechless with shock.

"Mary, you know I have become very fond of you," he explained. "I have been so alone since the death of my wife. You have been like a breath of fresh air. Your youth has made me feel young again. I will make you a devoted and loving husband, despite our age difference. I am financially secure—you will never want for anything," he promised.

My mouth was too dry to form any words. I sat silently while his words spun around in my head. Mama's eyes were bright with happiness. I never saw her so ecstatic. I thought of Joyce and my heart ached. I still loved her but I knew that Mama or Artie would never understand if I tried to explain. I thought about Patty and the women in California and Minnie. I knew that they would never understand about any of those women. I looked at Mama's happy face and remembered how tortured she looked when I returned from California and the girl's reformatory. I remembered how worried she had been when she thought that Joyce was leading me astray by taking me to bars. I hadn't seen her so happy in years—not since I had become a teenager and these strange mood changes had begun. I could never tell her that I wasn't attracted to men. I could never let her know that I found only women desirable. I loved her too much to break her heart anymore.

"What did you say?" I managed to ask Mama.

"I told Mr. Boyd that I thought it was wonderful. He will make a fine husband." Mama beamed.

A tight knot began to form in my stomach. I realized what a burden and disgrace I was to my Mama. I could see how proud she was that Artie Boyd wanted to marry me. I realized no one would ever want me. I had never seen her so proud. I felt ashamed for all the pain I had caused her. If I refused to marry Artie Boyd, I would only hurt her again.

I turned my head so that no one would see the tears that were escaping to betray me as I accepted Artie Boyd's offer.

Ruby rolled her eyes and sighed many times during the next two weeks while we prepared for the wedding. She didn't agree with Mama about the wisdom of this marriage but she wasn't going to argue the subject.

Sallyann gave me a wedding shower and all the relatives were invited. I opened the multitude of presents with a heavy heart. I wasn't sure if I could go through with the charade. Thoughts of suicide drifted through my mind as my only out, but I knew I couldn't go through with it.

Finally, the day of the wedding came. I dressed in the knee length white wedding dress that Mama and Ruby had picked out, and stood in front of the minister and promised to love and obey Artie Lewis Boyd until death do us part. Death—it sounded so beautiful now.

On the drive to Hot Springs, Arkansas for our honeymoon, I was very quiet. Artie tried several times to draw me into conversation. I responded with short, clipped answers.

"Mary, are you afraid of what is expected of you when we arrive at the hotel?" Artie asked.

I moved closer to the door and looked out the window.

"You have never been with a man?" he asked. I still didn't respond.

"Mary, I can assure you that I will never force you until you are ready. I am a mature man and understand the fears that a young girl may have. I wish that you would discuss your fears with me."

Now was my chance. I had to let him know. I had to explain. "No, I've never been with a man; I have never been attracted to boys," I whispered.

"That's understandable. Many young girls are attracted to older men," he assured me, misunderstanding what I was saying.

"No," I whispered even softer. I wasn't sure if he had even heard me. "No," I repeated. "I am not attracted to older men either. I am not attracted to men...period."

A wave of understanding washed over his face. His jaw was tense and his next words seemed to stick in his throat. He gasped several times before he choked out. "I see....Have you ever been with another woman?"

I couldn't meet his eyes. I turned and stared out the window. The rhythm of the telephone poles passing by my eyes created a hypnotic state and I didn't have to concentrate on my disgrace.

Artie didn't attempt any further conversation. When we arrived at the motel, I sat in the car while he registered us. Then we walked silently together to the room. After we set the bags down, the silence became unbearable. I looked for a subject of conversation but none came.

"I think I need some cigarettes," I announced, grasping at an excuse to run from the room.

"Oh sure," Artie said and handed me some bills and the car keys. "I think I saw a corner market when we drove in."

I looked at the keys in Artie's outstretched hands and my eyes moved to his face. He was giving me a chance to escape. This kind man was not going to keep me to my promise. I reached for the car keys. "Thank-you," I whispered.

He nodded in understanding and turned away to hide the hurt that I had seen in his eyes.

I used Artie's car to drive home. When I opened the door,

Mama stared at me in surprise. I ran into her arms, begging her not to make me live with Artie Boyd. "I promise not to be bad anymore," I cried.

"Be bad...." Mama wailed. "Mary Catherine, what are you talking about? I wasn't encouraging you to marry Artie Boyd because you were bad. I thought you were unhappy. I only wanted you to be happy. I was a foolish old woman. I thought if you were married and had children you would be happy. Children make you happy, Mary Catherine. You have made me very happy from the first day I got you...."

The rest of her words were drowned out by both of our sobs. She patted my hair lovingly and assured me that everything would be all right.

Mama returned Artie Boyd's rings and arranged to have the wedding annulled and we never saw Artie Boyd again.

My future was a continual concern for Mama. The idleness generated restlessness. I spent a lot of time away from home—in bars. The drinking seemed to ease the unhappiness. Mama was worried about the people that I was meeting in the bars. One of her main concerns was Bill. Bill was a friend of Ruby's for years. The spoiled son of rich parents, he had been given Arthur Murray dance lessons as a child and had frequented the Right Spot to dance.

I met him at one of the neighborhood bars. He was a quiet, gentle man in his mid-thirties—an educated man with a soft voice and soft manners. His soft red hair lay in curls giving him a feminine look. He usually got a lot of ribbing from red-necks at the local bars. Keeping company with me reduced the ribbing. Just being in the company of a female created the look of normality. Bill looked to me as his protector. After a few beers, I was quick to fight, to prove my masculinity. In red-neck bars someone is always ready for a fight. Bill realized I was gay and introduced me to the local underworld of gay life. He explained that bars called the 'Brass Rail' or the 'Carousal' usually catered to gay patrons. This was known by most gays in the 60's. On Friday nights we would meet and drive to Little Rock to the gay bars. The fights there were just as frequent because the locals would wait outside the bars until someone came out and then jump them. I learned to carry a gun

40

and a knife and had no hesitation about using either. I was in jail frequently for bar room fights.

Ruby would stop at a local cafe after work and buy fried chicken and RC cola to bring to me in jail. The local sheriff was a kind, understanding man who was completely enamored with Ruby's beauty and genuine concern for others. He fell in love with Ruby and years later they were married.

Mama and Ruby were concerned about my growing friendship with Bill. They were afraid I was falling in love with him and would be crushed when I discovered he wasn't interested in me.

"I don't know how to tell you this," Ruby confided to me in a hushed whisper, "but Bill is queer. He once said he would change if I married him, but...heavens, I couldn't marry a queer. I don't know what you see in him."

How could I explain that what I saw in Bill was a lonely man searching to be accepted. A mirror of my own tortured soul. A part of me wanted to laugh at her ignorance, but a part of me wanted to scream, "I know...I'm queer too," but I only sighed in resignation. "He's my friend. I enjoy his company."

Mama and Ruby's concern increased until, out of desperation, Mama arranged for me to go live in Missouri with Alice, Mama's older natural daughter.

Alice lived in a cramped trailer in a trailer court. I wasn't interested in enrolling in school or getting a job. There weren't any neighbors my age.

I established a friendship with Sweets, a neighbor in her thirties, who was a nurse at the nearby hospital. When she invited me to a game of miniature golf one evening, I accepted eagerly.

We had planned to pick up a friend of hers who worked at the hospital. We carried on a light conversation, laughing together at corny jokes as we drove to the hospital. "You just don't look like a Mary," Sweets teased.

"What do I look like?" I challenged.

"I don't know...have you ever had a nick name?"

"I used to play General Lee when I was a child. Sometimes my family kidded me by calling me General Lee...."

"I like that...I'll call you Lee," she announced as we pulled into the parking lot of the hospital.

A beautiful blond woman in her mid-thirties stood waiting for us. When she joined us in the car, she planted a wet, sloppy kiss on Sweet's lips. The two women broke their embrace and turned to me laughing. "This is my woman, Evelyn Queen, but everyone calls her Queen. Queen meet Lee...Lee meet Queen." Sweets watched my face for a reaction. "Are you shocked?" she asked.

"No." I said, "Just surprised, I hadn't suspected you were gay."

"Have you ever been with a woman?" Queen asked.

"I have always been attracted to women."

"I thought you probably were." Sweets laughed. "That's one of the reasons you're here tonight. We have a friend who we think is gay. She's married but miserable. We thought you might be her type. What do you say...want to meet her?"

I accepted the date. The friend's name was Juanita. She was forty-two and had three grown children. I was very comfortable with her. The four of us drove around talking and drinking beer, ending up at Queen's house for more beer.

After several beers, Queen and Sweets explained to Juanita their plans to 'turn her out.' An awkward silence followed. At this point in my life I already knew my powers of manipulation—how to be adorable to older women. With coaching from Sweets and Queen, Juanita and I shared our bodies with each other in blissful satisfaction. Sweets and Queen's suspicions about Juanita's sexual preferences were correct.

Over the next three days Juanita and I were inseparable. We drank, danced and went to bed together. We couldn't get enough of each other. Juanita decided not to go back to her husband, claiming he was cold and uncaring, and that she had never been as happy in her life as she was with me. We found a cottage to share and rented it.

While Juanita worked, I spent my hours at the local bars. My relationship with Juanita did not make me popular at the there. One evening as I was leaving one of the bars, I heard someone call to me. Three men whom I had noticed earlier in the bar and who had been looking for a fight then, now sat on the hood of a truck. They were dressed in jeans that were pushed down under their beer bellies and stained t-shirts stretched across their thick chests. Their sleeves were rolled up revealing tattoos on thick muscular arms. "Hey, little boy, does your mama know you're out alone?" one of the men called to me.

The alcohol had left me just as eager for a fight as he was. "No, she thinks I'm with your Mama." I called back. "You won't tell your Mama where I am, will you. I just can't keep up with that woman—I needed a break," I taunted.

"You dirty queer," the man cursed. "You dirty son-of-a bitch." He slid off the truck's hood. His buddies followed him.

I quickly realized the error of my words. Two of the men grabbed me by the arms. I could smell the stale odor of alcohol and tobacco on their breaths. The third began to pound his fist in my midriff. I kicked out in all directions landing a foot in his groin. This only fueled his anger. His blows became harder and aimed more at my face. I could feel the blood run down my face from a split in my cheek. My eyes began to swell. Just as I was losing consciousness, I could hear the sound of a siren and the screeching of tires as the police came to a stop. We were all surrounded and arrested for public drunkenness and creating a disturbance. Nothing was mentioned of the fact that I was one small woman against three men.

The bar room fights became a steady occurrence. One word or a bump against someone in a crowd—sometimes intentional, other times accidental—could create a fight. Some of the fights began and ended in the bar room, other times groups of men with their women in attendance would gather on the parking lot to give the queer what she had coming.

Alice had kept Mama and Ruby informed about my actions and the deviant characters I had chosen to spend my time with. When Mama's frantic letters and telephone calls begging me to straighten my life out were ignored, she gave up her house and moved to Missouri, renting a house close to Alice.

Mama was convinced that Juanita was responsible for the drinking and bar room fights that were now a way of life with me, but she was willing to allow the relationship to continue if I would agree to move in with her. Mama thought if I lived with her she could help me get a grip on my life. She even offered to let Juanita move in with us. Her efforts were all in vain—I ignored all her pleadings.

Juanita was obsessed with me. I was restless while she was at work and visits to the local bars were frequent. I soon found other women to fill the empty hours. Juanita would call home from work every day to check on me. If she called home and I wasn't there she would go into a jealous rage, leaving work to go to the bars in search of me.

I sat at a table one evening drinking a beer. A woman in her mid-thirties sat across the table from me. I looked at her soft breasts and decided that they would feel good close to me. "Want to dance?" I asked when the next slow song played on the juke box.

"Sure," she slurred—she had already had too much to drink. If she could stand up long enough to dance it would be a miracle.

I escorted her to the dance floor. We were mid-way through the dance when the woman's head was jerked back.

"You bitch." Juanita shouted as she slung the woman back away from me by the hair of her head.

I was immediately filled with rage. The woman could barely walk and Juanita was dragging her across the floor. I grabbed Juanita's arm and she let go of my female companion only to take a swing at me. I ducked and her fist cut through the air. I stood back up and swung at Juanita. My fist hit it's mark with a loud crack.

"Get the hell out of here," I heard the bartender yell. "I'm calling the law in thirty seconds."

I grabbed Juanita by the arm and dragged her to the car and shoved her in the passenger's side and slid under the wheel to drive home.

The screaming continued for the drive home. By the time we pulled up in the driveway the anger had died and Juanita was all soft and sweet.

I realized Juanita's anger was justified, especially after I had confessed to waking up next to a woman I didn't know in bed with me after a night of drinking.

"We need to get away from here," Juanita sobbed. "I can't keep on like this. It's driving me crazy. I worry about you all the time…who you are with. My husband came by the hospital today. He says if I don't come back to him he is going to kill you. I can't live without you. We have to leave," she cried hysterically.

"Relax, honey." I assured her. "He isn't going to kill me. He was just threatening so that you will go back to him. Everything is going to be okay." I promised. We ended up in bed and her husband's threats were forgotten.

Her husband kept his promise though. The sound of his squealing tires alerted us to his arrival. He stumbled out of the car in a drunken state, waving a small caliber pistol in the air. "Come on out you damn queer," he yelled. "Come on out and fight like a man." He laughed bitterly.

I started to the door, but Juanita stopped me. "You fool," she cried. "We are getting out of here."

We made our way out the back door and to Sweet's house, undetected by Juanita's enraged husband. Sweets gave us a .25 caliber pistol and we left her house to borrow a car from another friend of theirs. After drawing twenty-five hundred dollars out of the joint bank account Juanita shared with her husband, we swung back to our house. Juanita's husband had left so we hurriedly packed our belongings and put them in her car. After a quick telephone call to let Sweets know we were leaving the borrowed car in the drive we were on our way out of town.

We had no destination in mind. We traveled from town to town, stopping only long enough for gas or something to eat and more beer.

"God it will feel good to get out of this car," I said as we pulled into a truck stop in Florida. We had been on the road for what seemed like a century.

"Better give me some money to buy the gas with and pay for our meal," I reminded Juanita before she slid out of the car behind me. I resented the way she doled the money out to me in small amounts, as if she didn't trust me.

Juanita gave me a cold glare but reached in her purse for a twenty. "This should take care of everything," she stated stiffly.

I returned her cold stare with a stare just as icy. I didn't like the attitude she was adopting. We told the service-station attendant to fill the car up with gas and walked into the dining area of the truck stop.

We slid into a corner booth and a waitress came with the menu. We ordered steak, eggs and coffee. Our moods were somewhat better after we had finished our meal. "Go ahead and pay for the gas and meal while I go to the restroom," Juanita instructed and slid out of the booth.

I picked up the green restaurant tab the waitress had left and walked to the register. "Was everything okay?" the friendly waitress asked.

"It was fine," I answered.

"That's good." She smiled. "Your order was five dollars and forty-nine cents plus ten dollars for the gas. That comes to fifteen forty-nine," she said politely.

I handed her the twenty. "Keep the change." I smiled.

"Thank you," she cooed.

Juanita walked out of the restroom just at that moment. She took one look at the sticky sweet expression of the waitress and her temper flared. I rushed to her and guided her out the door before she could make a scene.

"What the hell was that all about?" she demanded.

"What are you talking about." I sighed.

"The cutie-cutie shit that was going on while I was in the restroom," she snarled.

"Nothing was going on. I just paid for the meal and gas."

"Oh, nothing was going on, huh. I bet you gave the little sweet thing a nice big tip too," she screeched.

"I tipped her, yes. Is there a law against that?" My was voice full of sarcasm.

"The standard tip is ten percent of the meal. Of course you have a different standard for tipping. You tip by the size of the tits. How much was her tip?" she demanded.

"Juanita. I am not getting into a screaming match with you because of something you imagined. If you don't want me to use your money then say so. I don't need your money. I will get out any time that you want me too."

Her mood immediately changed, her anger replaced by fear.

"No don't leave me," she cried. "I'm being unreasonable. I can't live without you."

The fight had ended as quickly as it began.

The drinking continued. I would go for long periods of time never sobering up and not remembering a thing.

Our fighting continued, Juanita always accusing me of 'whoring around,' screaming she wanted me out of her sight, but in the next instant she would be begging me never to leave her.

Occasionally we would pick up hitchhikers. On one occasion, a fellow we had picked up made a pass at Juanita. I became enraged and began beating him with the butt of the gun—almost beating him to death before Juanita was able to stop me.

When we put the stranger out he notified the authorities and our pilgrimage ended. Juanita's husband had reported the car as stolen and an APB had been put out on the car. We were stopped and, when I was frisked by the arresting officers, they found the pistol.

The federal authorities offered us a bargain. If I would plead guilty to the interstate transportation of a stolen motor vehicle then Juanita would be allowed to return home to her husband, who had agreed to take her back. It wasn't much of a bargain, but Juanita chose her husband over prison and I agreed to the deal. Perhaps it was poetic justice. I got sentenced to prison—Juanita got sentenced to her husband.

Ruby was present at the hearing. The judge sentenced me to six months to two years in the Federal Prison for Women in West Virginia. The tears streamed down Ruby's cheeks as she gave me a light hug. "Well, here is another mess you've gotten yourself into," she said in a sad voice.

CHAPTER 4

Alderson Federal Prison—Virginia, 1962-1964

"Fresh fish...fresh fish," chanted the crowd of women who had gathered to watch the new arrivals to the women's prison. I was unfamiliar with the slang words but I understood the meaning. Many of the women in the crowd tried to see the license plate on the transporting patrol cars; they hoped to recognize an officer from their home town, and so satisfy the desire for some contact from home.

The prison housed approximately six hundred and twenty women of all races. I was later to learn that racial segregation existed even in prison. If you were white, you mingled with white, the same for blacks and Spanish speaking inmates. You were considered an outcast if you mixed with a race different from your own. Each race had its leader, someone whom the rest of the women looked up to and took orders from.

I was escorted to central processing. There, I was finger-printed and mug-shots were taken for identification purposes to be filed in my records at the institution.

When the processing clerk was finished, the officer escorted me to an open shower where I was instructed to shower and was handed a strong smelling soap for de-lousing. I was then given a physical by the institution's nurse.

The next step of the initial processing was in the property room where a clerk issued me five pairs of army-surplus khaki pants and shirts, a peacoat, underwear, and shoes—all of which had been worn by previous inmates.

"What's your name, sweetie?" the inmate property clerk asked.

"Mary Dortch, but I go by Lee," I answered.

48

"Are you taken?"

"Taken...?" I looked at her.

"Yeah...taken...you got a woman? You are butch ain't you?"

"Oh," I said in understanding. "I have a woman on the street."

She threw back her dark head shaking her hair like a horse's mane. Her white teeth shown as she laughed. "Ha, you'll have several in here, sweety. My ol' lady was with me when we came in and within three weeks she got took...." When she saw the look of concern on my face she added, "Oh hell, I'll get her back when we are back on the street." She continued, "They house us according to your work assignment. Painters in cottage one, kitchen in cottage two, and so on like that. I'm in four. As you can see, I'm a 'fem'...maybe we can get together sometime," she added with a seductive wink. A wave of understanding washed over me.

As I was preparing to leave I saw a woman of Spanish origin who appeared to be segregated from the rest of the women. "Who is that?" I asked curiously.

"Oh, you mean Anna...Anna Alvarez." The girl craned her neck to see in the direction I was pointing.

"She is the assistant warden, Mrs. Mac's favorite. Her butch just left and she is depressed. They are letting her house in segregation until she gets her head on straight. Hey...I know you don't go for spicks? You stay away from them if you don't want trouble," she cautioned.

I was placed in temporary living quarters until I was classified to a work area. As I was being shown my cell, I met Anna Alvarez coming out of her cell.

"Hi. I'm Lee." I smiled.

She answered me with a cold stare and walked off.

The next few days, I spent trying to find out as much as I could about Anna. Each time I approached her I was rebuffed by the same stony stare.

"Does she speak English?" I asked another inmate.

"Yeah, she does...if she wants to. She is from New York— here on a drug charge. She is an addict. If you're smart you'll stay away from them spicks...if you run with them the whites won't have nothing to do with you...the blacks neither. If you fuck over one of them they will kill you—that one is hell to play with. Yeah, she speaks English if she has to but she won't have nothing to do with no faye." A faye I was to learn, is slang for Caucasian.

After a week of persistent attempts at conversation, Anna finally turned to me and said something in Spanish.

"I don't speak Spanish," I explained.

She laughed. "You will, *chula.*"

That was the beginning of our relationship. We sent kites, discreetly to avoid detection from the guards, back and forth. I made plans to move to cottage three where she was housed, but my plans were quickly squelched by the classification board. "You want to paint, you live in four," they told me. "If you want to live in three you get food service."

I couldn't see myself in the kitchen, so I agreed to four.

I was soon to experience the notorious Spanish temper. Anna was furious. "You fool! Now I will have to smuggle you in and out of the building. I told you to get assigned to three. I would've had it fixed so you could still paint," she wailed.

With the aide of other inmates to distract the guards, Anna was always able to smuggle me in and out of her cottage. But I was soon to experience the wrath of Anna's temper again when she discovered I had been with other women. When she confronted me, I denied it.

"If I didn't love you so much, you bastard, that lie would cost you your life. Be grateful the razor will not be put against your throat as you sleep," she smiled bitterly, and walked away.

I asked for a job change to the dairy and was housed near that work area. I went from female companion to female companion for several months. One day I looked up to see Anna walking to the dairy. "Mac allowed me to walk down here to talk to you. You can come home now."

I shook my head in bewilderment at her strange announcement. "I can't just move back. I'm classified to the dairy."

"No, you're not," she announced, triumphantly. "You're being re-classed today. I think you'll move to dorm three."

Anna's prediction came true. I was re-classed that day and moved out of the dairy to dorm three as a painter. We were happy until we made the fatal mistake of showing our affection in the open.

We were on the ball field, which was in direct view of the warden's office. The warden was entertaining a general and other dignitaries at that moment.

Anna informed me the next day that Mac had given her a choice. "You can either move back to the dairy or both of us move to cottage twenty-six."

Cottage twenty-six was a housing area for inmates the warden wanted out of sight. Inmates were locked in and only unlocked for three hours a day for food and work. It was nick-named the honeymoon cottage.

"Why?" I wailed. "I thought you had Mac in your pocket."

"Ha," she laughed. "Mac is the reason we have a choice. The warden wanted to ship you to the dairy right away."

So we moved to the honeymoon cottage.

Anna's time was getting short. I began to grow anxious.

"Do not worry, *chula*, we will be together when you hit the streets. I want you to experience my other love, smack, with me," she cooed, "You have learned to speak some Spanish and I will mark you as one of my people so you will be accepted."

She got a needle and ink and engraved a small dot in my forehead. "There, now you have the Spanish time mark," she announced.

Anna left soon after that day. Mac arranged to have Area Patrol pick me up and take me to the Admissions Building to tell her good-bye. Anna assured me we would keep in touch. Ex-inmates were not allowed to correspond with inmates who were still incarcerated but she promised me she had it arranged. "In seven months, *chula*, we will be together again." She smiled.

Officer Smith, an officer genuinely concerned for the inmates, would do small favors for them. She brought me Anna's promised letter in an unmarked envelope. After reading it, I realized I could not wait seven months to be with Anna. Being with other women did not ease the pain of being away from her.

My job as painter often involved working several stories off the ground. On one occasion, we were assigned to paint the exterior of

51

the buildings, some of which had steeples nearly ninety feet off the ground. None of us were ordered to paint the steeples but if an inmate wanted to volunteer, it was permitted. I volunteered.

As I stood on the edge of the steeple looking down, a part of me wanted to take the final step that would end my sorrow, but another part of me wanted to live...to be reunited with Anna. I became obsessed with getting out and being with her.

My obsession eventually changed to bitterness. Life was unfair. I hated everyone around me. On one occasion, I attacked another inmate, almost choking her to death before I realized what I was doing. "Why did you try to kill me?" she cried.

"Bitch" I cursed, "I didn't try to kill you, and if you tell the warden that lie, then I will kill you for sure."

"Lee. I won't snitch you out, but you need help," she whispered pleadingly.

My disposition worsened. My moods became more and more violent. When one of the plain envelopes that Officer Smith delivered to me from Anna had her address in the inside, I began to make plans for my escape.

I took a pair of four inch scissors that were issued to all inmates during their initial classification and broke them apart with a hammer from my work area. BJ, another inmate who worked with me on the paint crew, tried to talk me out of my plan. "Hey, you're too short. Don't do anything foolish."

Her words were useless. Finally she agreed to keep watch for me while I finished the shank, a homemade knife, if I would promise to take her and Mickey, a friend of hers, with me. I agreed to her request.

We made plans for sometime before Christmas, because I wanted to be with Anna before Christmas. On November 22, 1963, President Kennedy was shot to death in Dallas, Texas. Everyone was in hysterics. We agreed now was the time to make our break.

It was a biting cold Saturday morning as we sat watching, waiting for shift change to take our chance. Officer Smith crossed the upper campus parking lot. I called to her. She continued to unlock her car but slipped into the seat to wait while we joined her.

I jumped in and pushed Officer Smith closer to the passenger door, holding the shank to her throat. BJ jerked the back door open and Mickey jumped in the driver's seat beside me. In seconds we were on our way—our emotions charged by the excitement of our plans. We passed through the check point easily enough. The guard had already raised the bar gate before he realized that the car was being driven by an inmate. He gave the alert and the other guards were in hot pursuit immediately.

Road blocks were set up and for the next thirty minutes we passed through all of them and outran the patrol cars chasing us.

Officer Smith tried to talk us out of what we were doing, but BJ silenced her by bopping her on the head with a child-sized baseball bat she had found on the floor of the back seat.

Our final road block came as we rounded a curve. Blinded by an overhanging cliff, we were on top of the road block before we realized it was there. There was no time for decisions. "Crash it!" I yelled, and for the next three minutes all that could be heard were the sounds of metal hitting metal and glass shattering. Someone was screaming and then everything was over.

We were all pulled from the wrecked vehicle, Returned to the prison, we were put in isolated cells, pending the investigation of the escape, however we could call to each other from our cells.

A federal officer questioned us individually. "You realize that you could get the death penalty if Officer Smith dies," he informed me in a threatening manner.

"Dies?" I cried in amazement. "From what?"

"She was hit on the head and stabbed," the federal officer explained.

After the officer had left us and we returned to our cells, we called to each other. None of us were able to remember stabbing Officer Smith.

"I hit her in the head with the baseball bat, but it was only a light tap," BJ confessed. "You had the shank, Lee. Did you stab her?"

"I must have," I admitted. I was confused. I didn't remember stabbing Officer Smith and if I did, did I stab her accidentally or on purpose? Were those her screams I remembered hearing?

Officer Smith recovered and refused to press charges, telling the officers that she didn't believe we had intended to hurt her and that she didn't know which one of us had stabbed her or hit her on the head.

We all pleaded guilty and we were sentenced accordingly: Five years for escape, two three year sentences for assault and ten years for kidnapping. All of it was to run consecutively for a total of twenty-one years. In addition all of our good time would be forfeited and could not be regained.

The warden chose to separate us to avoid risking any future escapes. Mickey would remain in Alderson and BJ would go to the Federal Prison in Lexington, Kentucky. The warden had wired several institutions but no one was willing to board me. Finally the state penitentiary in Arizona agreed to take me.

Mary Dortch – age 15

At age 16 with a friend from reform school

Mary Dortch's wedding picture, 1962

1989 Lee sings a Christmas song she wrote herself– Tennessee Women's Prison

Lee and Lucy in Prison Law Library

Lee working a Law Clerk's office

Records
Form. #9

NUMBER 69777

W/ Dortch, Mary Catherine
Last First Middle
ALIAS: "Lee"

SEX: Female RACE: White COMPLEXION: Dark

HAIR: Dark Brown EYES: Hazel

HEIGHT: 5'6½" WEIGHT: 150

LAST ADDRESS: P. O. Box 133, Russellville, Ark.

MARKS, SCARS, TATTOOS: left arm scared; snake tatoo inside right hand; "Lee" on left arm; "Li. & Peace" sign on left arm.

MARTIAL STATUS: Single

PHYSICAL DISABILITY: None

DATE OF BIRTH: 3-20-43

PLACE OF BIRTH: Russellville, Ark.

OFFENSE: Murder 1st.Deg.& Arm.Robbery

SENTENCE: LIFE(5Co. Conc)

PROBATIONARY PAROLE DATE: 4-7-84 3/16/84
1BI-1/11-1815 -3-1-89 8-15-88
11-16-86

DATE OF SENTENCE: 11-15-71
DATE RECEIVED: 11-18-71
JAIL TIME: 2 Mos.3 days
COUNTY: Knox
COURT: Criminal
JUDGE: Joe D.Duncan
PLEA:

REGULAR PAROLE DATE: 4-7-85 - 3/16/85
1BI-1/11-1BIBL -3-1-90 8-15-89
11-16-87

PRIOR CONVICTIONS: ☒ None ☒ One
☐ Two or More

DETAINERS:

SENTENCE EXPIRES: No Exp. Date

NOTIFY: Mrs. Lillie Rone (mother)
P. O. Box 133, Russellville, Ark.
Phone: 967-3376
(501)

TYPE OF CUSTODY:
_____ Date
_____ Date
_____ Date
_____ Date

LOST 360 Days G.H Time 9-12-79
LOST 1460 DAYS GOOD AND HONOR TIME 5-29-80
6-24-82 530 Days Good Time If

PAROLE BOARD HEARINGS:

Standard Form 507
(Revised August 1954)
Bureau of the Budget
Circular A-32

U.S. GOVERNMENT PRINTING OFFICE : 1961 O—587879

CLINICAL RECORD	Report on _____ 507 Notes
	or
	Continuation of S. F. _____
	(Strike out one line) (Specify type of examination or data)

(Sign and date)

October 28, 1969: Dr. Elizabeth R. Strawinsky - Clinical Director
AJ   CLOSING NOTE AND SUMMARY OF THE CLINICAL RECORD
                   This 26-year-old, separated, white, Catholic female was discharged
from the Hospital today as improved, into the custody of the United States
Marshals, to : return to the Federal Reformatory for Women at Alderson, West
Virginia, to complete her sentence. A letter of notification was sent to her
aunt, Mrs. Lillie Rone, P.O. Box 133, Russellville, Arkansas.

          She was admitted to Saint Elizabeths Hospital for the second
time on February 21, 1969, under the provisions of Title 24, Section 212 of U. S.
Code, as a transfer from the Federal Reformatory for Women at Alderson, West
Virginia, where she was serving sentence for interstate transportation of a
stolen motor vehicle, assault and kidnap of a Federal Officer and escape from
the Federal Reformatory for Women at Alderson, West Virginia.

          She was born March 29, 1943, in Russellville, Arkansas, the
oldest of 2 girls. She had several frictions with authority in school and was
resentful and hostile. Her delinquency problems reportedly began when first
menstrual periods occurred. During these periods she withdrew to her room, avoided all
social contacts. She was described as fat, sloppily dressed and not accepted by
peers she admired. In 1960, she spent 6 months in a juvenile institution. She
began homosexual practices early in childhood. She completed the 10th grade and
was expelled in May 1959 after threatening a girl with a broken coke bottle.
She was involved/row over narcotics and ended up in reform. school for 6 months
where she disrupted the other girls because of her homosexuality. There after
she got into a series of trouble and gave herself up. She was arrested for armed
robbery in June 1959 and was observed at the State Hospital in Little Rock,
Arkansas. In 1962, she married a man/52 and was unable to live with him after two
weeks and claimed to have filed for divorce the same year. In 1962, she was
charged with violation of the Dyer Act and received 2 years at the Federal Reformatory
for Women at Alderson. In 1963 she was evaluated mentally and diagnosed as an
emotionally unstable personality, severe. On November 1963 she assaulted and kid-
napped a Federal Officer escaping from the reformatory, they were captured when
they crashed through a roadblock and she was prosecuted. In October 1964 she was
taken to the California Institution for Women where she became assaultive with a
female correctional officer and forced her to release her homosexual partner,
escaping over the fence accompanied by this female in July 1965. In August 1965
she was returned to serve a 1-year to life sentence. She continued her behavior
pattern involved with homosexuality and self-destructiveness. In March 1966 she
was accepted at the Oregon State Penitentiary where it was found that she has had
the impulse to kill people since _____first person being her aunt.

PATIENT'S IDENTIFICATION (For typed or written entries give: Name—last, first, middle; grade; date; hospital or medical facility)	REGISTER NO.	WARD NO.
DORTCH Mary C.	89,473	JHD
Saint Elizabeths Hospital	REPORT ON _____ or CONTINUATION OF 507 Notes	

(Sign and date)   L4

DIAGNOSIS: 301.58 HYSTERICAL PERSONALITY. SEVERE
                   XXXXX(Lesbianism.) HOMOSEXUALITY.
            302.00
      CONDITION ON DISCHARGE: IMPROVED.

                              Elizabeth Strawinsky
                              Clinical Director

Judge orders inmate's release from isolation

U.S. District Judge John T. Nixon today ordered the release from solitary confinement of an inmate isolated by Tennessee Prison for Women officials for "therapeutic purposes" following a Jan. 4 suicide attempt. The order came in a lawsuit filed by Mary Lee Dortch, the inmate, who charged authorities unlawfully deprived her of clothing, blankets and communication with the outside world. Nixon issued a preliminary injunction today ordering officials to transfer her to DeBerry Correctional Institute and to start a thorough medical and psychiatric examination of her within the next 10 days. Nixon ruled that the inmate's 90-day "behavior modification plan" was a form of punishment rather than therapy. He said it violated prison regulations since officials ignored her right to treatment. Ms. Dortch, who has a history of prison violence and suicide attempts, is serving five concurrent life sentences for armed robbery and murder.

10/27/90 Tennessean

Inmate sues, says she's forced to shave

By ROCHELLE CARTER
Staff Writer

A Tennessee Women's Prison inmate, claiming public embarrassment and emotional suffering, has sued a prison official for allegedly making her shave her face "like a man."

Mary Lee Dortch, 47, serving a 30-year sentence for a 1971 Knox County murder, four counts of armed robbery and one count of aggravated arrest, said Correction Capt. Stevenson Nixon forced her to shave. She wants $10,000 in damages.

Dortch said in the lawsuit she has been "the subject of jokes and taunts as a result of the forced shaving."

"If it were reasonable for a female to shave, then some form of aftershave and conditioner should be provided as is so for men," said the suit in Davidson County Circuit Court.

"However, to order a female to shave is cruel and unusual punishment and should be against policy."

Dortch said she has had a little hair on her face since she was a child. Because it was shaven off it has grown back thicker.

A copy of the state Department of Correction dress code for prisoners attached to the suit states "females are not permitted to cultivate or attach beards and mustaches." Men are not allowed to wear cosmetics, but can grow their hair long.

"The plaintiff has worn this small amount of hair since youth," the suit said. "To shave it would cause it to grow, thus 'cultivating' it, which the policy prohibits.

"Never has this female been told to place a razor on her face to remove a natural growth of hair that is nowhere near like a beard."

Department of Correction spokesman Brandon Maloney said the department could not comment on the suit because officials had not seen it. Nixon could not be reached for comment.

Dortch, who has been incarcerated for almost 20 years, has a colorful history with the state prison system.

In 1973, Dortch escaped with a guard as hostage, using a broken pair of scissors as a weapon. She was recaptured 40 minutes later.

In 1978, she overpowered another guard and held her hostage with a razor blade at her throat for 30 minutes until she was allowed to talk to the warden.

In 1983, she allegedly overdosed on some type of drug.

The following year, she filed a lawsuit in U.S. District Court against the use of solitary confinement for prisoners who had not broken any rules, but the suit was later dropped and she was transferred to DeBerry Correctional Institute. ■

CHAPTER 5

Arizona State Prison—Florence,Arizona 1964

I was taken early one morning—shortly after my twenty-first birthday—to Bluefield, Virginia by Officer White, a male officer from Alderson. I was held in the local jail there until the plane departed that would take me to the Arizona State Prison where I was to serve my twenty-one year sentence. It was a life-time as far as I was concerned.

Officer White was kind when he escorted me in public, by allowing my jacket to be draped in a manner that covered my handcuffs discreetly.

Later, on the plane, when the stewardess came for our drink orders, he laughed when I looked at him questioningly.

He said with empathy in his voice, "Go ahead, Lee, it will probably be the last drink you'll have for a few years."

I drank the two little bottles of whiskey that I had ordered. Officer White gave me his two little bottles as well.

Two United States Marshals met us at the airport and escorted us to the state prison. While the officers alerted the prison authorities of our arrival, I studied the area.

The men's prison was on one side of the road and the women's prison on the other side. A solid wall, approximately twenty-five feet high surrounded the women's prison. The gun towers of the men's prison were situated to observe both prisons.

A steel gate, called a sally-port, was opened to admit us. Once inside the fence another steel gate and fence encircled the area. Doberman pinchers guarded inside the fences. I was later to learn that they were cared for by Indian Joe, an inmate from the men's prison who had a life sentence. He was the only one who could get near them. I tried to approach one of the dogs only to freeze in my tracks as his vicious snarl warned me not to come any closer.

"No one can get near them," the officer told me. "They are trained to attack and kill."

I laughed, "So if I make it over the first fence, the dogs, then the wall...what next?"

"You die," the guard said. His expression was stoic revealing nothing. "There's a desert out there. No one has ever made it out of here alive."

I was beginning to understand why this prison had accepted me when no other would. An uneasy feeling crept through me like frosty fingers.

After my papers had been processed, I was taken to an isolated cell where new arrivals were locked down until they were medically cleared.

I was to stay there for fifteen days with only one set of clothes, a tooth brush, and cigarettes. The lights were turned off at night. The cells were four steps under ground. The dark, cool underground cells were an invitation to snakes to come in from the desert and prey on the rats and mice that infested the cells. Thus, they were dubbed the "snake pits" or "snakes" for short.

The next morning the nurse came for me. I was escorted to the infirmary and given a physical. I was then brought to the men's prison where pictures and finger prints were taken. After I returned to the women's prison, I was taken to the warden's office for orientation. The warden sat behind his desk rigidly, staring blankly at me. "Sit down," he said. "I have a few things to say. You will not interrupt me. After I am through, you may comment, if you still want to."

He was a small man, but I sensed he was small only in stature. His speech gave evidence of his strength—his power. "They tell me you are called Lee. You think you're a real bad ass. Well, I want you to know you can take a hostage here anytime you want. But hell no, we won't open the gates for you. You will be shot. If the officer gets killed also, well they know the risk when they take this job. Try me, if you want. Others have...others have died," he challenged me with a grin that did not reach his eyes.

I looked into the man's eyes and I could sense the danger in them.

After the fifteen days in isolation, I was housed with other inmates. There were two housing units, one for trustees and another one for inmates.

The housing unit was composed of a motley crew of women housed in an open dorm. I met a girl, Sybil, who was twenty-four years old but whose hair was snow white. I learned she had had flaming red hair that had hung to her waist. It had been shaved and she had been strapped in the electric chair. At the final moment before execution, her death sentence had been commuted and her life had been spared, but her hair had grown back white...from fright.

I also met Winnie Ruth Judd, a notorious ax murderer from the thirties whom the press kept public for over forty years. She was called the Tiger Woman. At the time of Winnie's crime, she had been living with two nurses who worked at the same medical clinic as herself. Neighbors had heard screams coming from the apartment. Two days later Winnie had taken a trip by train to Los Angeles, carrying a large trunk and a small trunk. When the baggage room employee helped her load them in her car, he noticed dark red fluid dripping from a corner of one of them and demanded to know what was inside—he suspected poached deer meat.

Winnie sweetly told him the keys to the trunks were in the car and she would get them, but used the time for her escape. The baggage clerk managed to get her license number.

When the authorities opened the trunks they found the dismembered bodies of the two nurses. An alarm went out for Winnie's arrest. She surrendered five days later, after a public appeal from her husband whom she had been separated from for some time.

The papers rumored bisexual and homosexual activities had been common at the apartment and the slaying was a result of a lover's quarrel. Winnie had insisted she had killed in self-defense, claiming she had been shot in the hand during a struggle between the women. The prosecution pointed out that no one had seen any wounds on her hand until two days after the killing, prior to turning herself in. She was found guilty and sentenced to hang but the governor granted her stay and a sanity hearing just seventy-two hours before her scheduled execution.

At the hearing the Tiger Woman put on a show to beat all shows. She clapped, yelled and laughed at the jury. She jumped up once and tried to fly out the window. Winnie's mother testified that she herself was feeble-minded and that her daughter had been "more or less insane all her life." Her father produced a family tree that traced insanity back over one hundred years to Scotland. Winnie emphasized the point by ripping at her hair and trying to pull off her clothes. She was finally removed from the hearing room and was ultimately judged insane and sentenced to life imprisonment in the state mental institution.

When she arrived at the institution, Winnie no longer acted crazy. She was quiet and plotting. She fashioned a dummy of herself, put it in her bed and escaped. She was found some days later, brought back and tightly confined. It did no good—over the years she escaped seven times. Following one of her escapes to California, the governor ordered her returned. Doctors ruled Winnie was perfectly sane and she was sent to prison. She had been there twenty-five years when I arrived.

My youth brought out her maternal instinct. She said I reminded her of herself when she was younger and she took me under her wing.

She loved to make me laugh and would tell me of her escapades while we played cards. She had a knack for making the heinous sound humorous. She was a small woman with wiry gray hair that gave her a witchy appearance. A prankster, she would cackle with a witch laugh after pulling one of her tricks on another inmate. The new admissions usually received the brunt of her pranks.

One of the showers was angled in a position that could be viewed from the officers' desk. The older inmates knew to use the other showers but when a new admissions mistakenly used the shower, Winnie would alert everyone in hearing distance—bidding them to join her while she watched the unsuspecting inmate shower—making comments about her body.

Her humor—no matter how sick—was a relief for the hardship

we all endured. These women were harder than any I had ever met in my twenty-one years of life. Their environment had made them hard. Sorrow was a constant thing. It settled over you like a shroud. It sucked away the essence of yourself so that you felt dead.

We worked seven days a week. There were no religious services. If you believed in God you asked for his mercy or prayed for death when you lay in bed at night, exhausted from the hard work.

My job assignment was five days a week in the laundry and two days as a runner. The heat from the laundry combined with the Arizona heat sapped my strength leaving me weak and exhausted. The lack of strength made the runner's job unbearable. A runner carries mail, commissary, supplies, whatever is needed from one area to another. You are assigned a number and when your number is called you move it as fast as you can.

My job was later changed to runner five days and yard work two days. The yards were irrigated to keep the grass growing on the hot desert by using a fire engine and fire hoses to water the areas. It took three people—using all the strength they could muster—to hold the powerful hoses. My guts would hurt from the strain of the hard work.

We were supervised by two male guards. I had seen them take their fist to women who refused to work. The temperatures would reach 115 degrees and women would faint from the hard work in the heat—only to be left lying where they had fallen.

I witnessed many cruel acts. Once, an inmate was beaten by an officer for stopping to light a cigarette while scrubbing the sidewalk with a toothbrush. On another occasion an inmate had her appendix removed and five days later was put back to work. She would pass out repeatedly only to be covered with a blanket and left lying in the hot sun. No one was allowed to stay in the dorm during work hours—no matter how sick.

Mental cruelty was as common as the physical cruelty. The generators that powered the electric chair, also powered our institution. Once when an inmate's husband was electrocuted, the lights dimmed. The woman's screams haunted the other inmates for weeks.

None of the socializing went on the way it had in the institutions I had been in previously. You were too tired for anything but sleep. Even if you had any urges, they were quickly squelched. Your movements were too controlled. We were housed in open dorms, divided by cubicles with waist high partitions. Two yellow lines were painted on the floor. You followed the yellow line to your cubicle and went in. You were subjected to punishment if you stopped along the way or went beyond your cubicle. Winnie referred to the lines as the "yellow brick road." Her bed was directly across from mine and she would call to me just before going to sleep. She had a twisted sense of humor and would poke fun at the day's events. The guards viewed her as crazy and shied away from her. She was free to say and do whatever she wanted— the rest of us didn't have the courage to try.

The environment bred evil and sadistic behavior. On one occasion, I asked a woman who professed she loved me, to prove her love for me. She took a lighter and burned her right arm. I delighted in the sick, perverted sacrifice.

My moods grew darker, full of hate. I became defiant—failing to perform my work assignment; deliberately ignoring when my number was called to make a run. Winnie would have the other runners make the run to cover me. They would claim that I was in an area where I couldn't hear my number.

On an impulse one day, I was bound and determined to prove the warden wrong in his statement that no one had escaped. I was about three feet up the fence when I noticed a guard passively watching me.

"Aren't you going to stop me?" I questioned.

"Hell no...you'll stop when you get four and one half high," she answered. I looked at her with a puzzled expression and she motioned to the armed guard who stood in the tower. His rifle was aimed at me—with orders to fire when I reached the four and one half feet mark.

I dropped to the ground. The reality negated any dreams of escape.

I was spared the physical abuse the other inmates were subjected to because I was a Federal prisoner but the abuse still went on about me. Sometimes, I felt it was just as hard to watch it as to be subjected to it. There was an ever present bitterness inside me. It was my only protection from the cruelty around me. My moods grew more and more violent.

I wanted to strike out in anger at everyone. The violence in me finally erupted when another inmate leaned across me in a seductive manner. The woman considered herself desirable and had been making advances at me all week. I considered her a slut and was repulsed by her advances. When she leaned across me I started beating her...all my frustrations channeled into every blow I struck. I was finally pulled off her by two male guards from the men's prison—the female officers were not supposed to interfere in a fight. They were instructed to call for assistance from the men's prison.

I was escorted to the snakes and thrown in. I lay on the cool floor for about fifteen minutes, trying to get a grip on what had just happened, before the door was opened again.

Two male guards, followed by the warden, entered. The two guards grabbed me on each side and the warden hit me in the stomach with his balled up fist. When I bent over, he continued the crushing blows to the back of my head. Then he began to kick me with his boots until my knees buckled and I fell to the floor. I lay there in a crumpled, bloody heap. My mouth and nose were bleeding and swollen.

"You son of a bitch," the warden snarled. "The next time I will kill you...if I have to lay your body across the fence and say you were killed in an escape attempt, I will. It's a cardinal sin to strike one of my officers. Hit another one and you're dead! This time I'll starve you until you wish you were dead."

With that, he turned on his heels and marched out. I dragged my broken body to the cot where a stiff wool blanket lay. I covered my head and wept. What was he talking about, I wondered.

For the next two weeks, I was served three pieces of bread every morning through the wicket. I drank water from the sink to keep my stomach from cramping. After two weeks I began to get one meal a day with no salt, sugar, or coffee.

One evening an inmate who was in another cell was able to use a piece of the plastic from her institutional mattress to slip between the door and unlock her cell. She then proceeded to unlock all the other cells that housed inmates for punishment. We couldn't go any farther than the hall but we enjoyed the brief moment out of our dungeon-like cells before the guards were alerted. We were all ordered to return to our cells and our doors were welded shut.

The silence seemed to accentuate the darkness of the cell. As I would lie on my cot at night I could hear the soft, whispering sounds in the dark as the snakes slithered across the floor of the cell, or the soft struggling sounds of a rat who had fallen victim to one of the desert snakes.

I learned from the nurse that, supposedly, I had thrown a chair during the fight, hitting one of the female officers before she could lock herself in the control room and call for emergency assistance—she was limping now.

I stayed in the snakes for sixty-six days before my door was broken open and the female superintendent came in. She instructed me to bathe and then she would take me to the Warden's office.

"The officer who claimed you had hit her with the chair has admitted to lying," she explained. "She was aware you were a federal prisoner and was in hopes that the Feds would compensate her for any injuries you inflicted."

"The warden has sent for you. He won't apologize but he will shake your hand and tell you to get back to work. I suggest you hold your temper and shake his hand," she cautioned.

"Hell no," I shouted angrily. "He has had me beaten and locked in this dark cell for sixty-six days...I haven't been able to bathe or to see daylight. I won't shake the bastard's hand."

"Don't be stupid. He'll have you thrown back in the hole. I've contacted the Feds and explained what has happened. I witnessed the beating...I'll be leaving here to find another job and I don't want you killed before the Feds get here."

I still refused to shake his hand. I was returned to the hole. Four days later, I came out of the snakes and shook his hand.

The federal officer arrived and the warden brought him to the dining room where I was eating.

"Do you want to see this man?" the warden asked.

"It doesn't matter if she wants to see me or not," the federal officer spoke up. "She will see me. Will you leave us alone please?"

I looked up at the warden. He was grinding his jaws in aggravation but he turned on his heels and left us.

I ate while the federal officer talked—if you left food on your plate you were subjected to punishment.

"The Federal Department wants you housed, not mistreated. You will be transferred soon," he explained.

I looked up from my plate and glanced over at the warden who was glaring at us while we talked.

"You should have brought someone to transfer me when you came because I will be dead in a few days," I said coolly.

The federal officer looked in the direction of the warden. "No, he won't hurt you anymore. I have already informed him you had better be in perfect health when you are picked up. I don't know when, but it will be soon," he promised.

After the federal officer left, the warden joined me. "I know you will be leaving soon. If you are ever free, then you better take the long way around Arizona...because if you come here as a state prisoner you are dead." With that he turned and walked off.

I was picked up in two days and taken by plane to California where I would again be boarded as a federal prisoner in a state institution.

CHAPTER 6

California Institution for Women, Corona California
1964-1966

I was transported by a different Federal Marshal but he was just as kind as the one who had brought me to the Arizona Prison. He was a sturdy man in his mid-forties with a touch of gray at the temples.

"Lee, we won't get to Corona until around eight o'clock tonight. The office personnel will have already gone home, so I'm going to leave you at Terminal Island overnight. It is a minimum federal prison so you will have to stay locked down. I'll stay at a hotel and we can drive to the women's prison in the morning," the Federal Marshal explained on the plane.

"I wonder what this prison will be like," I asked.

"The conditions will be a lot better then the Arizona Prison," he promised.

"Hell would be better than that prison," I added.

He laughed, "Yes, from what I read in the report I'm sure it would. This prison is a small town in itself. Over seven hundred women are housed there. I've seen it and I think you will be comfortable there. It has a large commissary and dining room. The food is good. They have many more work areas."

The marshal's words were true. The next morning when we arrived at the prison I was overwhelmed at its size. I was quickly and efficiently processed in and assigned a living area until I had completed the classification.

We were housed in single rooms, dormitory fashion. New admissions were housed in a different dorm from the main population. We were free to walk around but restricted to the area. I met many of the other inmates who were waiting to be classified.

I was one of the youngest inmates there—twenty-one. The prison usually kept women over twenty-five. The younger women were sent to another prison, but because of my escape record, it was too much of a risk to house me at the medium-security prison.

I had lost a considerable amount of weight because of the sixty-six days spent in the snakes. My appearance gave little evidence of the female that I was.

Of the many women in this prison, only approximately fifty were butches. Many of the women began to send me kites. Some were at my door frequently offering to clean my room or do my ironing in the hopes that I would consider one of them to be my "ol' lady." I enjoyed the attention that these women bestowed on me. I received sandwiches made especially for me and smuggled from the kitchen and extra linens stolen from the property room.

I learned that Los Angeles and San Francisco have always been in competition with each other—there was no exception inside the prison system. The women from Los Angeles hated the women from San Francisco and visa versa.

If I showed too much attention to one of the San Francisco women then the Los Angeles women would be upset. If I showed too much attention to a Los Angeles woman then the San Francisco women became upset. I enjoyed the competition.

The staff was not pleased with the stir I created among the women but they did not resort to the abusive treatment that I had been subjected to in Arizona.

I adjusted well to my environment but memories of the women I had left in that horrible prison in Arizona and the cruel treatment they would still have to suffer haunted me. In an effort at improving their prison conditions, I wrote a letter to the Federal Bureau for Prisons.

I received a memo through my counselor that all the federal prisoners had been removed from that prison and that the Bureau of Federal Prisons had no jurisdiction over the state prisoners. I had been the only female prisoner. The male prisoners had been removed shortly after I left.

The frustrations of not being able to do something for these

65

poor women angered me. I slammed my fist down on the counselor's desk. She moved quickly to call for assistance, but when she saw I had control she settled back down. My reputation for violence had preceded me.

I was resentful of all authority but realized I was there only on probation and that Corona had not formally agreed to house me indefinitely. Any show of disruptive behavior, mental disturbance or violence and I would be immediately turned over to the United States Government to find housing elsewhere. I lived in fear of another prison like Arizona so I behaved.

My counselor assured me that if I felt upset, I should inform someone. I could volunteer to be locked down until I felt I was in control and it would not be held against me. It would not be a disciplinary lock down.

I continued to behave myself and showed no signs of violence. I had one minor discipline when a "frozen count" was called and I was in another dorm. It took several minutes for me to be smuggled out and I was late for count. I was given five days lock down.

California finally agreed to keep me as a permanent resident and I breathed a sigh of relief.

A few weeks after I arrived at Corona, I saw a woman on the tennis court. She had dark brown hair that was so dark it was almost black. She was short with a shapely figure. Her legs were firm and tanned—evidence of many hours on the tennis court. I thought she was very attractive and wanted to get to know her better. I began following her whenever I saw her. She finally stopped one day and turned around. "Why are you following me?" she asked.

"Because I want to find out your name," I answered arrogantly.

"It's Carol. Now stop following me," she ordered and turned to walk away.

I ran to catch up with her. "You must be new here," I said. "I haven't seen you around."

She laughed at my feeble attempt at further conversation. "No, I'm not new but you must be or you would know that I work in the clinic."

"Oh…well, maybe I will see you then."

"Maybe," she agreed and walked up the stairs to the dorm we were standing in front of.

I turned to walk back to my dorm when Donna, a Los Angeles girl, caught my arm. "What are you doing talking with that stuck-up bitch?" she asked.

"Why do you say that?" I asked. "She seemed nice."

"Yeah, if you like killers," she sniffed and proceeded to fill me in on Carol's criminal history. "Her name is Carol Tregoff. She has a life sentence. Her case was on television and in the newspapers for months. There was even an article in a magazine. Some people say that the show *The Fugitive* was based on her crime.

"Her family has a lot of money and she was a model. Then she met Dr. Raymond Bernard Finch, a big-shot doctor and fell in love with him. She started working in his office to be near him while she got a divorce from her husband and he got his divorce from his wife. But in California when the grounds for divorce are adultery, the courts usually award all the property to the innocent party instead of dividing it equally. If the doctor sued for divorce, Mrs. Finch would get all the property including her husband's interest in a medical center—plus she was demanding heavy alimony. If she won, Dr. Finch would have been left broke," Donna explained, watching my face for a reaction, then continuing on.

"According to the newspapers, Dr. Finch and Carol testified that they had hired a petty crook named John Patrick Cody to make love to Mrs. Finch in an effort at obtaining compromising evidence against the doctor's wife. Later, according to Cody, Carol offered him fourteen hundred dollars to shoot Mrs. Finch. He claimed that she stated, "'If you don't shoot her, Dr. Finch will...or if he won't, I'll do it.'

"Anyway...Carol and Dr. Finch testified that they drove to the Finch home for a conference with Mrs. Finch. There was a shot, and Mrs. Finch lay dead on the driveway with a .38 bullet in her back. Dr. Finch's version was that during an argument his wife had pointed a gun at him and he had taken it away from her and tossed it over his shoulder. The gun had gone off and shot his wife. But the prosecution claimed the lovebirds had come to the Finch home with a so-called murder kit for the purpose of killing Mrs. Finch.

67

The first plan, according to the prosecution, called for injecting an air bubble in the bloodstream and if that failed, injecting a lethal dose of sodium seconal. An alternate plan, the prosecution contended, involved driving the unconscious woman over a cliff in back of the house. The prosecution contended the shooting was deliberate and presented scientific testimony that the woman was in flight when shot."

Donna stopped to catch her breath and I nodded for her to continue. "When Dr. Finch took the stand, big fat tears ran down his face and he gave a heartrending version of his wife's last words to him after the accident. They were: I'm sorry...I should have listened to you...I love you...take care of the kids.... The press thought it was a novel defense, almost as though the victim was apologizing for being killed. Nevertheless, the doctor's testimony was effective, resulting in a hung jury after eight days of deliberations.

"Finch and Carol, who had not spoken a word to each other throughout the trial, were retried a second time, and again the jury failed to agree. On the third try, Dr. Finch was convicted of first degree murder and Carol of second-degree murder. Both were sentenced to life sentences.

"As they left the courtroom, Dr. Finch tried to kiss Carol but she turned away. The girl in the mail room says she still gets letters from him but sends them back unopened." Donna finished and looked to me for approval for the information she had just shared with me. I shrugged my shoulders and walked off silently, leaving Donna standing open-mouthed at my lack of interest in the gossip.

I began to see a lot of Carol. I would wait for her to come out to the tennis court or to sun bathe and strike up a conversation with her. She was despised by most of the inmates because her job as the Doctor's aide gave her access to keys to the medicine cabinet. She had refused several requests to steal drugs for other inmates.

I asked her one day, "Why? After all you are an inmate also."

"Yes, Lee, I am," she said sadly. "I remember that everyday. That's why I don't allow my family to send me clothes to wear. I prefer to wear these shapeless state uniforms so I'll constantly remember I am an inmate. But I also am a nurse. I am devoted to saving lives. It gives me pride when I am able to assist Dr. Pierce deliver a baby to one of the other women. I could never give someone drugs knowing what it could do to them. If the other inmates hate me, then I'm sorry."

I admired this woman greatly. I noticed she never used profanity. I questioned her about this and she answered me with a smile. "How I feel about myself is important to me. I will not change for these inmates. Profanity is an example of a small vocabulary."

Carol taught me to play chess and once when she caught me reading a book she considered smut, she took it from me. "Come with me."

She motioned and we walked to the library where she picked Harold Robbin's *The Carpetbaggers* from the shelf. "It's got sex and violence but it's done tastefully...read it."

I read it and I enjoyed it. She gave me a list of other authors whose books I would enjoy. I had never been interested in reading but Carol taught me to love books. She told me that if I found a word I didn't understand to look it up in the dictionary and use the word until I was accustomed to its meaning.

As physical attraction was the only kind of relationship I had ever known with a woman, I confused her friendship and the admiration I held for her with physical attraction. She kissed me maternally and said, "Lee, I love you but I am not in love with you."

She was always full of praise for me, never ridiculing me. She promised, "Lee, if you keep on behaving yourself the way you have been, I'll see if I can get my family to help you."

I wanted to be as near Carol as possible. When I came up for re-class, I asked for the job at the car wash and to be moved to the same cottage she lived in. There weren't any empty rooms available but there would be one in five days. I wanted to be in the same dorm as soon as possible.

"Can I sleep in the hall for five days?" I asked. The re-class board agreed and I moved the few belongings I had, storing them in the room I was to occupy. I slept in the hall.

I began wild plans for escape. I was convinced if I helped Carol escape, she would be so grateful she would fall in love with me.

I got an address for a place in Venice, near Los Angeles, from a woman called Faggot. She was called that because she looked very mannish but dressed feminine. Faggot made me promise to take Karen, an inmate who had a life sentence with no parole for drug trafficking. I promised but did not say there would be three of us—me, Karen and Carol.

I made friends with the third shift officer—making her coffee the first night I was in the dorm. By the third night she said, "Lee, where's my coffee. I've been here twenty minutes."

Later that evening, I told the officer I saw a towel thrown out of the wicket. This was a signal that the guard was needed by one of the inmates.

"Go see what she wants." The officer instructed.

I went to Karen's door. "Get ready," I whispered. "Do you have sheets torn up to tie her with?"

"Yes, let's do it fast before I lose my nerve," she answered in a shaky whisper.

I returned to the office. "She wants some aspirin," I lied to the officer.

She got the aspirin and started down the hall. I grabbed the table leg that I had hidden under my mattress and tucked it in my waistband.

She handed Karen the aspirin through the wicket. I reached my left hand around her and covered her mouth. I pulled the table leg out from my waistband with my right hand. "Be quiet and you won't get hurt," I hissed. I could feel her tremble. "Unlock the door," I demanded.

When the door was open, I pushed her in and ordered Karen to tie her up. "Wait here," I said while she was in the process of tying the woman's legs.

Karen looked up, her face full of fear. She asked, "Where are you going?"

"Don't worry, I'll be back. Just finish what you are doing," I instructed. She returned to the task of tying the guard.

I grabbed the guard's ring of keys and raced down the hall to Carol's room. I could see her through the wicket lying in bed reading. I pecked on her door. She looked confused but came to her wicket.

"Carol, I love you. We are leaving." I confessed in a rush of words.

"Oh no, Lee, what have you done?"

"Hurry Carol...get ready...I've already tied up the guard."

"Lee...darling...I can't leave. I'll make parole in two years. I wish you had told me what you were planning before you did this. My god, Lee, have you lost your mind? It's too late now to turn back. Go on without me. Run! Write me—use my mother's name," she cried.

I had to tear myself from Carol's door. This wasn't what I had planned. I didn't want to leave without her.

I turned away. Karen was just coming out of her door. She closed it and locked it automatically. We raced out the front door, locking it behind us. Our hearts seemed to be pounding in our throats as we moved cautiously to the side of the building, then to the chain-link fence with the razor wire strung across the top.

Our first attempt at climbing over the fence failed because the razor wire kept snagging our clothes. We both dropped back down.

"Pull off your clothes and shoes and throw them over," I ordered Karen. I did the same—embarrassed at standing in the well-lit yard in my T-shirt and panties.

This time we were able to go through the razor wire. We dropped down on the other side of the fence. Our skin was torn and bleeding from the razors but we were free. We grabbed our clothes and ran for the fields.

"If you see a light, lie flat," I instructed Karen as we pulled our clothes back on. We continued to run—slowing to a walk only while we caught our breath. When we came to a house with a 'For Sale' sign in the yard, we went into the empty barn to hide.

It started to rain and we trembled together from cold and fear. Later, as Karen slept, I thought how I had planned on Carol being here with me and how foolish I had been not confiding my plans to her. I finally slept a fitful, restless sleep.

When we woke it was morning. We ached from the cuts but we were free. We laughed together hysterically, bragging about our 'big escape.'

Finally, we made our plans. We would need food, clothing, and transportation. We needed to find out if the newspaper had our descriptions. We later learned that an APB had been put on us less than two hours after we had escaped. Flyers had been sent out the next morning.

We were able to find a house where the owners were not at home—on vacation we presumed because of all the newspapers in the driveway. I broke a window with a rock and succeeded in unlocking the door.

After a quick survey of the icebox, liquor cabinet and clothes closet, we agreed we were in luck. We ate and both of us took a long leisurely bath. The male member of the family wasn't very tall and his clothes fit me nicely. Karen found a skirt and blouse to her liking.

By the time we explored all the rooms and had taken advantage of the owners' uninvited hospitality, I had consumed a considerable amount of their wine. Karen became frightened by my wild threats and challenges to the absent hosts.

"I'll kill them," I boasted.

When she got the chance, Karen hid the shot gun she had found in the bedroom, under a mattress to keep me from finding it and hurting someone.

But I had found a knife in the kitchen and slipped it in my waistband.

We found a set of car keys, and a quick inspection of the garage rewarded us with the use of the owners' second car. Soon we were on our way to Venice.

After I sobered up, Karen told me how wild I had acted when I was drunk, and how frightened she had been. I apologized to her.

When we arrived in Los Angeles, I called the telephone number I had gotten from Faggot. A 'gay boy' came to pick us up. After wiping the car's doors and interior clean, we left it parked with the keys in it.

The boy drove us to Venice, a play city of gays, thieves and prostitutes. I was able to make some money as a look-out for a couple of small-time thieves.

This wasn't the life I had planned on. I was restless and bored. I called Mama and Ruby to let them know I was okay, in case they had been notified of my escape. Mama answered the phone. "Mary, we have been so frantic...where have you been?" she cried.

"Mama, I want to come home," I begged.

"If you come home, they'll shoot you, Mary. The FBI have been here. You have to turn yourself in. I told them you wouldn't hurt anyone but they won't listen. They said I didn't know you." She began to cry. "Please, Mary...please go back."

Ruby took the phone. Her anger assaulted me. "Don't you care about Mama? You've scared her half to death. How much are you going to hurt her before you kill her. Go Back!" she order. "If you don't go back, don't bother calling here again. You're killing Mama."

I promised to go back and hung up the receiver before the tears could escape. I found Karen in the gay bar we frequented, and explained what I had to do.

"You're crazy," she said, her voice full of bewilderment.

"I promised Mama," I explained.

Karen could tell from my tone of voice that I couldn't be talked out of my plan.

"We can get passports and start all over," she said in one last, feeble attempt at stopping me.

I looked at her sadly and picked up the telephone. "Leave here, Karen. I'm calling the police."

The nasal twang of the operator's voice sounded in my ear, "Operator."

"Give me the police, please," I said into the receiver.

"Is it an emergency?"

"No stupid, I just want to talk to them," I snapped.

The next voice was that of the Culver City Police.

"You're looking for Lee Dortch," I announced arrogantly.

"For what?" the policemen drawled lazily.

"Check!" I ordered.

He left the phone, then returned quickly, his tone more urgent. "Yes, we are...have you seen her...just tell us where she is...don't go near her," he cautioned.

"She must be dangerous," I teased.

"She is!" the officer assured me. "Where is she?"

"You're talking to her," I laughed, thrilled by toying with him. "I'm at the Golden Jukebox Night Club. I'll be here for ten more minutes...after that, I'm gone."

I walked over to a table and sat down. Karen remained at the bar, watching me in the mirror. She had dyed her hair so she looked nothing like the woman who had escaped from prison with me.

Within minutes I heard a siren. Four officers burst into the club, their weapons drawn. A hush fell over the place like a thick storm cloud.

One officer shouted, "Lee Dortch, raise your hands above your head and stand up. Everyone else, don't move."

I realized that they didn't know which person I was. I slowly raised my hands and stood up. The officers quickly surrounded me and handcuffed my hands behind my back. They frisked me, removing the knife I had carried since finding it in the vacant house.

As I walked past the bar, I could see Karen in the mirror. I could see tears in her eyes but I dared not turn my face.

On the way to the police station, I slipped my handcuffs off—a trick I had mastered years ago—and passed them to the arresting officer when he opened the car door. Jumping back he drew his weapon and held it on me while the others snapped them back on.

"I can log the deadly weapon we found on you."

I understood his meaning. "I can explain how you were negligent in putting the handcuffs on."

His male pride won, and the deadly weapon was never mentioned, nor the handcuffs.

I pleaded guilty to escape with force and violence. The federal authorities said since the state pressed charges, any action they took would be double jeopardy. I received one year to life, which would run consecutively to my federal sentence.

I was transported back to the California Institution for Women and placed in segregation. The classification board denied my work and housing request unless I would tell them where Karen was. I refused, so when I was released from segregation, I was sent to Bonnaberg Cottage and put in the dorm on close custody.

I was miserable in Bonnaberg. Wilson Cottage—where Carol was housed—was across the campus. I felt so alone and ashamed of my foolishness. My pent up frustrations were vented in fits of rage. My moods were dark and stormy. I hated being back. My promise to Mama was forgotten. I knew I had blundered and the self-loathing only added to my inner rage. I began to take my anger out on those around me, yelling at the staff and doctors. My actions were becoming unbearable.

On one occasion I snapped at Carol when she tried to talk to me about my behavior. My action hurt her feelings, and she refused to talk to me again. This only added to my loneliness and frustration.

I was indignant that Carol refused to love me. At first I was embarrassed at my foolish action, then I decided to get even with her by going with other women. I was arrogant enough to assume Carol would care and be hurt. When Carol refused to respond to my childish behavior, I became angry—angry at her for not loving me enough to be jealous, and angry at myself for my foolishness in thinking I could force her to accept me.

After dinner one evening, Mickey—a girl who had been coming on to me for days—asked me to come to her room. I agreed and she said she would shower and meet me later. I consumed a large amount of hooch—homemade wine—before going to Mickey's room.

It wasn't the romance Mickey had counted on. The hooch intensified my rage and Mickey was the object to vent my rage upon. I began hitting her with a desk lamp. Somehow Mickey succeeded in getting me to stop the vicious assaults, and I looked at her pale, pain-wracked face and the odd angle of her arm and realized what I had done. Full of remorse, I rushed from the room.

On my way out of the cottage, I passed a guard. "You need to check on Mickey in room sixty-seven," I called and rushed on.

Inside Patrol found me wandering around the yard and took me to the psychiatric treatment center in the small golf cart that they used inside the prison yard.

I was placed in an empty cell. A Chinese toilet—a hole in the floor—was used for human waste. A thick plate-glass window was used to observe me. I was given a shot of morphine to calm me.

75

The next day a police officer came from San Bernardino and informed me that Mickey had claimed she fell. He scowled, "She is either scared to death of you or devoted to you."

I didn't comment; my mind was sifting through the ruined state of my life.

None of the other women would make any statements or admit to knowing anything, so no charges were ever filed.

I was locked down. Other inmates were allowed to wait on me but my isolation increased my loneliness. I knew Carol would have to come and attend to my medical needs so I began cutting my arms, legs and stomach. I was surprised at the gratification I got in the self-mutilation. It was a method of atoning for the guilt and self-loathing. Carol would plead with me to stop.

"If you cut yourself again, Lee, I won't come," she warned.

I didn't believe her and when I cut myself again and she sent someone else to see about me, I felt rejected.

After weeks of self-mutilation I realized that no matter what I did, Carol was not coming. I accepted this reality with the fickle attitude of youth. There were more fish in the sea; she wasn't the only woman in the world; I really didn't like the stuck up bitch; the list was long.

I began to plan to get out of isolation and back into population, but the staff had different plans. My sudden change in behavior confused them and they had no intention of letting me out.

I knew my only recourse was to force them into admitting they couldn't handle me and insist that the Feds house me elsewhere. I had Winnie Ruth Judd as a role model. I began screaming at the staff and inmates who were allowed to come near my cell. I would throw things in my cell and call obscenities to anyone passing.

The inmates who had been allowed to come near me were forbidden. I then refused to talk to any staff members. If it was necessary to answer a question, I would write a simple answer on paper.

The self-mutilations continued. All attempts at removing objects that could be used for inflicting self-punishment from my reach were in vain. On one occasion a flashlight had been left by a staff member in the hall outside my cell. I tied my clothes together and using them as a lasso, threw them down the hall and dragged the flashlight closer. When I had secured it, I broke the glass that covered the bulb and used that to cut my wrist.

On another occasion, I jammed the lock to my cell with paper and set fire to my blankets. It took the officers longer than I had anticipated for them to burst into my room. The room became unbearably hot. I soaked some blankets in the sink and sat in a corner with my head covered until the staff could break the lock open.

I suffered some lung damage from the smoke inhalation and all my blankets were removed.

Medication was used in an attempt at controlling my violence. I resisted all medication—throwing it back at the staff administering it.

Morphine shots were finally forced on me. I began not to fight the shots and looked forward to the good feeling the shots gave me.

The violence continued until California finally said "enough" and contacted the Federal Department.

I was told I was going to Oregon State Prison.

CHAPTER 7

Oregon State Prison—Salem, Oregon 1966

I was again transported by a Federal Marshal to another state prison. I was full of mixed emotions. I feared another prison like Arizona and was sorry to leave the California Prison but I was hopeful of another prison with the freedom of movement like Alderson or Corona—where I could start all over.

We drove from the airport to the outskirts of Salem, Oregon where the State Prison was located. We passed the men's prison before we arrived at the women's prison. It had a twenty-foot high block wall around it and looked like a medieval castle. The women's prison was around the corner of the wall, and the catwalk and gun tower were situated to observe both prisons. The women's prison was enclosed with a chain-link fence. Razor wire was strung across the top of the fence.

As I looked at this prison a feeling of doom gripped me.

I was processed in and taken to the Warden's office. The warden was a small, white-haired man with steel gray eyes. He ran both the men's prison and the women's prison. He spoke softly. "Miss Dortch, you will be processed like anyone else. I have no fear that you will escape. My guards are trained well. They keep a sharp watch and are excellent shots. I have no intentions of keeping you segregated. If you want to get out of prison you will behave yourself and I will give you the chance to work toward your freedom. We will be able to finish your processing once your federal records arrive, but I see no reason why you can't begin orientation now."

I listened quietly. I sensed in him a man just as deadly as the warden in Arizona, despite his words of encouragement. I was sent to medical where I saw the nurse and she reviewed my medical history and told me that I would be scheduled to see the psychiatrist.

"Why?" I protested.

"Some of your medical records arrived and the psychiatrist had noted that you are to continue the treatments California had planned for your possible seizures," she explained.

"I wasn't aware I had any seizures," I answered.

"Your records reflect that you had an abnormal E.E.G." she added.

I thought on this piece of information. "Would that be a test where wires were all over my head—I remember going somewhere one day and having that done."

"Yes, that was it. The medication prescribed is mysoline—250 milligrams, three times a day."

The psychiatrist explained that there were new medications to help people like me, and he intended to try some of them. He wanted to see if a control could be found to help me stabilize my violent behavior.

In this prison everyone was locked down the majority of the time, with an hour break three times a day. I soon realized my foolishness in manipulating the system in order to be moved. I had been hoping for another prison with more freedom of movement; all I had gained was less freedom.

I had no intention of staying. I knew the Feds would move me if the prison could not handle me and I knew my skill at terrorizing the staff with violent behavior. I intended to use it again to force still another move.

My second week at the prison I used a razor blade from the commissary to inflict superficial wounds on my arms. This was the excuse the doctors needed to initiate their experiments in mind control drugs. A series of drugs was ordered. Massive doses of thorozine in a time release capsule were among the drugs I was given. Many of the other drugs caused me to hallucinate and I lived in fear of what I might see when I turned around. I pleaded with the doctor not to give me any more of the medication but he would pat my hand solicitously and smile, "Perhaps the dosage is too high, we will decrease them."

The lower dosages did reduce the hallucinations, but I began to

79

have periods when I couldn't remember what I did the day before or even the hour before. These memory lapses frightened me and added to my confusion; I was disoriented most of the time.

The doctor would recount conversations I had held with him, conversations I had no memory of. In these conversations I had apparently revealed a desire to kill my mother and I had urges to kill little animals. I look back at it now and wonder if these revelations were not the guilt I carried for my natural mother's death and the death of the kittens that Sewell had initiated, guilt that was twisted into madness by the drugs being administered. But at the time these revelations left me even more frightened. I had never felt any urges to kill my mother and I had always loved animals. The doctor assured me he had help for me—more medication.

The heavy medication left me lethargic. I couldn't move without effort. I had to force myself to go from the bed to the bathroom.

All my pleadings to stop the medication were ignored. I knew I had to get away. I lived in constant fear of the medication so I decided to resort to more drastic measures. On a break in the day room I pretended to lose control and erupted in a violent rage. I began throwing chairs in the day room, breaking glass and causing the other inmates to run screaming in terror down the hall for a staff member.

When the guards arrived, they encircled me and I was escorted to the hole. My medication was increased. Bread and water were ordered as my meals for six days a week. Sundays I was given a regular meal. I refused the Sunday's meal until another inmate was able to let me know that a message would be hidden in the food. I began accepting the meal and would search the food for the message. A tiny pencil and cigarette papers were included to return messages. I would eat some of my food, leaving enough to bury the return message in.

In one of return messages, I requested a razor blade to trim my hair. The next Sunday, the razor arrived and I trimmed my hair. Then I placed the razor on the wall by putting Vaseline on it. It clung there unnoticed.

The warden informed me that Ruby and Mama had called and both were concerned because I had not written. He added that if I would work toward improving my behavior, I would be allowed three cigarettes a day, four letters mailed out, and three books per week.

My concern for Ruby and Mama forced me to agree to his conditions and for the next two months my behavior improved. The warden ordered for me to be moved to my regular room. I realized that my period of calm had lead the staff to believe that the medication had stabilized my behavior and that this prison intended to keep me. I had to do something to cause them to change their plans.

I again pretended a fit of rage and tore up my room. I was immediately moved back to segregation.

The razor blade was still clinging to the wall, waiting for me. An hour later an officer was concerned because I had gotten quiet and came to check on me. She found me unconscious, my wrist sliced—this time more than superficially.

I was rushed to the men's infirmary. When I came to I was surrounded by officers and male inmate aides. One of the aides gave me a cigar—he didn't smoke cigarettes and explained that he had assisted in giving me a transfusion, assuring me that I would be okay. I received this piece of news with mixed emotions. I wasn't sure if I wanted to be okay.

I stayed at the men's infirmary until the next day. I enjoyed talking with the inmate medical aide. He filled me in on his life history. He had been a medical doctor on the streets until he got a murder charge. He didn't explain how and I didn't ask.

The next day, when it was determined I was in stable condition, I was escorted through several gates back to the women's prison. There I was locked back into segregation.

The female superintendent came to talk with me. "We are taking all of your privileges away," she explained. "No mail; no books; and no smokes." She had barely gotten the words out when I attacked her, ripping her clothes off and hitting her in the face. She ran, screaming from my cell while I hurled obscenities after her. Then I began to laugh—wild, hysterical laughter; growing louder and louder rising to an insane pitch, an imitation of Winnie Ruth Judd.

The cell window was protected by a mesh cover. I began to break this window, ripping through the mesh. A female officer came to the wicket.

"Lee, they said I have to take your clothes and blanket," she announced in a voice intended not to cause me any further excitement. "I know how modest you are, if you don't give them to me then the male guards will have to come and get them. I asked them to let me see if I could get them from you first...I hate this Lee, but it's ordered, so it's up to you."

I certainly wasn't going to allow myself to be undressed by male officers, so I gave her my clothes and the blankets from the cell.

It was late October; I quickly felt the cold from the window I had broken. I huddled in the corner farthest away from the window. The room grew from cold to arctic and before morning I prayed for death to come and release me from my misery. The tears would escape and slip down my face, only to be wiped quickly away when I heard an officer approaching. The officer would open the wicket and peek in.

"Are you okay?" she would ask.

"Hell no, I'm freezing to death," I yelled and added a string of obscenities.

"Lee, you know I can't give you a blanket, but here, drink this," the officer offered.

"What is it?" I demanded.

"It's chloral hydrate—it will help you sleep. It will make you drunk enough to stand the cold." She laughed in an effort at easing the tension.

I drank the bitter liquid. I didn't sleep but it did make me drunk and I was able to bear the rest of the night.

The superintendent came to my cell the next day. She leaned down and spoke to me through the wicket. "Have you learned your lesson?" she asked maliciously. I spat in her face. She slammed the wicket quickly.

"Lee Dortch...I'll take your blanket forever and you can damn well freeze," she screeched.

She returned three days later, a smirky tone was in her voice. "Lee Dortch, I'm going to open the wicket and you had better not spit on me."

"Open it bitch, I wouldn't waste spit on you," I hissed.

She opened the wicket.

"Lee you will be leaving here tomorrow. We need to move you to your room to pack your things," she explained. "Don't be foolish and try anything. Just stay calm until the marshal gets here," she warned. A feeling of triumph washed over me. I had succeeded. I would once again be moved.

"You just don't want the Feds to see how you are treating me," I accused in an effort at masking my glee, "but, okay, move me...where the fuck am I going this time...China?"

"You're going to a hospital for the insane," she answered.

The panic began to rise in me. I hadn't planned on this. I didn't want to go to the insane asylum. I only wanted to be moved to another prison, somewhere that I could move around...somewhere like California or Alderson...not an insane asylum.

"Why...I'm not insane," I exclaimed. "Do you think I'm insane?"

"Don't you?" she answered sadly.

CHAPTER 8

St. Elizabeth Mental Hospital, Washington, D.C.

I was transported by plane to Washington D.C. with a federal marshal. From the airport we drove to St. Elizabeth Hospital.

I thought of the movie "Snake Pit." It was a story of a young girl who was mistakenly committed to an insane asylum. Horrible pictures of shock treatments and criminally insane inmates attacking the young girl kept flashing through my mind. My stomach was a tight knot of fear. I wanted to cry but I didn't want the Federal Marshal to see me. I turned my head to the window and wiped the tiny tear that had escaped and was running down my cheek.

"You'll probably only be there for thirty days," the marshal assured me in an effort at easing my anxiety.

His words did nothing to quiet my fears. My heart raced with anxiety. I was afraid of the unknown. More movie scenes of insane asylums from Lon Chaney and Boris Karloff movies flashed through my mind. My mouth was too dry to answer him.

When we arrived at St. Elizabeth, I wasn't expecting the grassy lawn with park benches setting under thick maple shade trees enclosed by decorative fence.

An attendant at the gate directed us to Cruvant, which was the division I was to be assigned to. As we found our way, I noticed people walking around freely, some with nurses, some laughing and holding hands. I was later to learn there were over nine miles of grounds belonging to the hospital. It was not restricted to convicted felons, but was a government hospital where service men and women were treated as well.

When we arrived at Cruvant, I was escorted through a small locked screen door to Ward "D", where a nurse asked the routine questions on admissions. She asked me if I knew the date, year and how many fingers she was holding up. The clinical director had already gone home but the nurse assured me I would see her the next day.

I was taken to a small, plain room and instructed to strip and shower with a strong smelling, disinfectant soap. A stout, muscular female attendant sat placidly guarding me until a shower became empty. I meekly obeyed the attendant's orders to undress and shower. I hurriedly washed, trying to ignore the burning shame of standing naked in the stream of water from the shower. I tried to shield my body from the woman's prying eyes by crossing my arms protectively across my chest. I wanted to cooperate with the nurse in all areas. I didn't want them to think I was insane and keep me forever.

After the shower, I was given clothes and the nurse arranged for me to have some money from my account.

"You are allowed to have twenty dollars a week on your person. If you behave yourself you can move up to "B" status and go outside and to activities in other buildings," she explained as we walked from her sterile white office down the corridor.

I tried to listen to questions being put to me by this woman but fears of what lay ahead pounded in my brain, drowning her words. My pulse quickened and a tight knot returned to my stomach. Somewhere the sound of a woman's high-pitched scream echoed thoughout the corridor, causing the hairs on my neck to stand up.

As we entered the ward area, I looked around at the confusion and fear. I remembered the screams and shivered. Women were sitting bolt upright in bare chairs, or sitting or lying on the floor. Some were moaning while others were in a vegetable-like state. I looked at the staff that were in attendance. The ward nurses and orderlies had big, hard muscular bodies. The windows were covered with thick, steel mesh. I could feel the panic rising in me, smothering me.

After the nurse had briefed me on what to expect, she indicated a day room where I could go and play cards or watch television. She then showed me a ward-type sleeping area.

"Pick one and tell the other nurse where you'll be sleeping," she instructed.

I looked at the rows of beds. Many of them did not have sheets, and the plastic, institutional mattresses were rolled back. I assumed that meant they were empty. I wondered if I was evaluated on how socially adjusted I was by my choice of beds—I chose the corner one.

In the bed next to me was an older woman with gray wiry hair that framed her face like a wild animal. She sat in a stone-like state with her left arm raised above her head.

"Hi," I greeted.

She did not acknowledge my greeting—not so much as a blink of the eyes. I did not attempt any other form of conversation.

After I had deposited my belongings on the cot and advised the nurse of my bed selection, the nurse finished orienting me. I was informed that everyone was required to shower at least three times a week.

"If you don't, then the nurse will have to shower you," she explained.

I glanced at the unkempt women around me with their hair matted and hanging in their faces, and assured the nurse that was not a problem. Mama had instilled cleanliness in me as a child and I liked being clean—I enjoyed showers.

The last of her instructions were about the group sessions each morning and the group activities.

"Dr. Stravenski insists that everyone attend these sessions for one hour every morning. You do not have to speak, but you do have to attend. After that, your time is your own. There are many social events planned for the evenings. You are encouraged to participate, but they are not mandatory. There are many dances and parties on some of the other wards and divisions. If Dr. Stravenski feels that you are mentally stable enough, then you will be allowed to attend these, as well."

I slept well that night and attended the nine o'clock morning session where I met Dr. Stravenski. She was a tall, slim woman who radiated concern and compassion. I was immediately comfortable with her. I later found her to be very intelligent and astute about her patients.

Most of the women in the session remained silent. After some coaxing, others began telling of their fears.

A short, overweight woman in her mid-thirties began to talk to the group. "I have an intense fear of balloons, red balloons are scarier than the others," she explained.

"You know the reason for this fear now, don't you, Alice?" Dr. Stravenski asked.

"Yes, I know the reason, but I am still afraid of balloons," Alice continued.

Dr. Stravenski remained silent and the woman continued to talk. "When I was six years old, my brother and I were returning from a birthday party at a friend's house. We had had a wonderful time and had a piece of birthday cake and a balloon on a string to show our mother. My brother started running with his balloon when he came in sight of the house to be the first to show our mother our balloons. He ran across the street without looking for on-coming cars. He was hit by a truck and his little body lay in the street before my eyes. His balloon came to rest beside his body. I was so frightened that I couldn't move. I didn't realize that the balloon was a symbol of my brother's death but I was always afraid of balloons after that. As I grew older, the fear intensified. When ever I see a balloon I start shaking and my pulse races. The fear is somewhat better now that I know why I am afraid of balloons, but it is still hard to control the shaking...I'm working on it," she smiled and sat down.

As the weeks passed, I began to relax. I learned that the high piercing screams came from behind locked, steel doors and I wasn't as afraid of them as when I first arrived. I began to take comfort in the confusion and fear around me. I was no longer set apart from everyone for being different or strange. I tried to understand the behavior of some of the patients.

I would watch the woman in the bed beside me. She would sit for hours with her arm extended in the air—only moving it when a nurse or attendant would put her in a different position. On one occasion, I held my arm up in the same fashion to see how long I could hold it there. A few minutes later, my arm began to ache and I was forced to bring it back down. I made several attempts at getting her to talk but they all failed. I tried getting her to blink her eyes by slapping my hands together in front of her face but she did not respond.

I really began to enjoy the group sessions. I could dramatize these sessions in my mind. I would conjure huge, flaming pictures of Jack Nicholson in *One Flew Over the Cuckoo's Nest*.

I began to wear a knit cap like the one he wore in the movie and nick-named one of the nurses "Nurse Ratchett."

Dr. Stravenski appointed me ward chairman. My duties were to encourage other inmates to participate in the group sessions by asking them their opinions. I realize now that Dr. Stravenski was encouraging me to communicate with others and also keeping me occupied.

I insisted on a secretary to keep the minutes. Dr. Stravenski granted my request and another patient was appointed to keep minutes. Dr. Stravenski always appointed a different minute-keeper. I noticed on several occasions that these patients would be writing when nothing was being said. I didn't think much about the fact that the minute keeper was always a patient who was reluctant to participate in the sessions and perhaps was relating her feelings in writing. I did wonder if the doctor's evaluation of me was drawn from the notes that the minute keeper kept. Now, I realize that these notes were more useful in evaluating the minute keeper.

"The session is called to order," I announced, using my shoe in the manner of Nikita S. Khrushchev as a gavel to call the meeting to order. I am sure that my antics were nerve racking for Dr. Stravenski, but she sat silently taking notes.

"Donna is going to be the minute keeper today. Does anyone want to volunteer to be first?" I asked the group of patients who sat around the table in the session room.

No one responded to my request. "How about you, Susan? You never talk. Do you want to tell us why you won't talk?" I asked.

Susan was a quiet, mousy girl who kept her head down and never looked anyone in the eye. If you spoke to her she would hurry off in the opposite direction. She looked at me now in terror, as if I had just insisted that she jump off the Empire State Building. I felt sorry for her and moved on around the table to someone else.

There were patients with a variety of mental disorders hospitalized here—young, old, service women and veterans.

One patient was always quoting the law. It was said that she had been the prosecutor who had sent a man to the electric chair. Later when he was exonerated—*after* he was executed—she lost her mind.

Through these sessions, I learned about the other patients. The majority of them were paranoid schizophrenic. They would kill you for laughing, if they thought you were laughing at them. Most of them appeared normal, but many had murdered for some trivial reason.

They were usually kept calm by medication but there were occasional flair-ups. I had been there a week before I first witnessed what a paranoid schizophrenic is likely to do.

I was playing cards in the day room, when Celestine leaned over and whispered in my ear that the nurse was out to get her. She had imagined that she had seen the nurse look her way and whisper with some other patients. I ignored her. She continued to glare in the nurse's direction.

"Well, she won't be able to hurt me, I can tell you that, Lee," she whispered. With that, she left the day room unobserved by the rest of the patients and nurses in the day areas.

Celestine went to her room where she kept her crocheting material and returned with a long lethal crochet hook. Some instinct caused the nurse to ward off the steel hook by throwing up her arms for protection, but it was in vain. The crochet hook pierced one of her eyes before she could protect them from the assault.

Her piercing scream echoed throughout the day room and the rest of the patients huddled in fear as six male nurses wrestled with Celestine. After twenty terrifying minutes the nurses were finally able to sedate her and take her to STR (Special Treatment Room) to be restrained and kept heavily medicated.

The nurse lived, but she was blinded in one eye.

Celestine's medication was changed and she was released from STR two weeks later. She never mentioned the incident, nor did any of the other patients or nurses. Everyone was in quiet agreement that it had happened because Celestine was ill.

I was uneasy. The reality of the danger that was constantly around engulfed me. To push the fear from my mind I began to make light of my surroundings. I joined forces with some of the patients to out-wit the staff. At times, patients who were capable of it, took great pleasure in codes and secrets. Some of our secrets included smuggling drugs from ward to ward. Some patients who had regular visits were able to have drugs brought to them by their visitors. We would tie a bundle of bills to a string and drop it from our window to the ward below us. In a few minutes we were able to pull the string up and a small bag of heroin would be tied on the end of the string. Another method of drug smuggling would be to put the drugs in the pockets of shirts that were to be ironed by another inmate.

On another occasion, I established PRF (Patient Relief Fund). Its purpose was to relieve the patients of their funds. I would play on patients' paranoia by instilling a fear that the nurses were out to steal their money, then instruct the patients to draw money from their accounts. For a fee of five dollars, I would keep up with their money for them. It was a lucrative business. However, we were subjected to routine body searches by staff members looking for drugs and I was caught with an unusually large amount of money on my person. Our secret organization was abolished.

The hardest thing for me to deal with was the forced medication. It instilled fears in me that I could not handle. When I was on the medication, I was afraid of everything. Small fears would be intensified to phobias. I had always been shy in public places but now sometimes I would be terrified to eat in the dining room.

I remember once being in the dining room and overcome by panic. I picked up my fork and my hand started to shake so that I couldn't eat. I was frightened and thought I was having a seizure. I waited a little, thinking it would go away. Someone asked me why I wasn't eating and I began to think everyone was looking at me. This increased my panic. I wanted to run from the dining room, but I knew that would only draw more attention to myself. Somehow, I made it through the meal and returned to the ward.

Another time, while in a group session, I was gripped with sudden panic that I would not be able to talk. When I stood up to bring the meeting to order my mind went blank. I couldn't remember any of the patient's names or what I was supposed to do. I tried to remember but all that came to my head was a bunch of jumbled scraps of thought. I got dizzy and my hands started to shake. I dropped the shoe that I used as a gavel.

Dr. Stravenski spoke to me privately after the group session. I was afraid to tell her these things. I was afraid of what she would think it all meant—afraid that I was truly insane. I liked this kind, caring woman too much for her to think I was insane. I wanted to tell her everything in the hopes that she could make it all go away, but I was afraid that if I did, she would be repulsed by my secrets. I remained silent.

I began to think I was constantly being watched and it left me full of distress. When I thought I was being observed, I would experience a variety of symptoms which included involuntary shaking of the hands, fainting, perspiration, dizziness, weakness in limbs, and hyperventilation.

Sometimes I would go for long periods of time heavily sedated with several types of drugs. I don't think the hospital considered us guinea pigs. All the medication that was being administered had already been thoroughly tested on guinea pigs and rats and was now approved for humans. It was the sixties when behavior control through drugs was a new field. The proper dosages and reaction to combining different medicines were not thoroughly tested. In recent years, psychiatric doctors have found that the use of behavior control medication on patients with mental problems must be carefully done, and large dosages for long periods of time are never used. Combinations of drugs could cause psychosis, convulsions, paranoia, memory loss, hallucinations, and many more side effects.

I was given 1,250 milligrams of Thorazine a day combined with Elival, an antidepressant, and Mysoline, for seizures, on a regular basis for years. Doses of Placidyl and Chloral Hydrate were administered periodically. The effect of the massive dosages and the combination of drugs was devastating. Fifty grams of Thorazine will knock a grown man out but I would force myself to remain on my feet, afraid to give in to the medication—afraid of the nightmares that came with unconsciousness. The memory loss and depression along with the hallucinations were just as frightening as the night-mares. I would experience hysterical outbursts and more tranqui-lizers would be administered. I would try to refuse my medications but they were forced on me. It was given in liquid form or mixed with juice to ensure that I couldn't hide it under my tongue. At times, I would hold the liquid in my mouth to spit out later, but the staff soon learned of this and a nurse would follow me around for thirty minutes or longer until I swallowed it.

The boredom added to the depression. We had weekly activities but they soon grew dull and repetitious.

On the weekly outings, hundreds of patients from all wards were escorted in a long line to the movie theater. As we moved from the hospital area to the movie theater in what I called our Thorazine shuffle, I was overcome with a fear for my mother's death. I had just received a letter and she had mentioned she wasn't feeling well because of a cold. I became overly concerned. I was sure that she would become seriously ill and die and I would never see her again. I felt an urgent need to be at my mother's bedside. I walked, undetected, away from the group. After I had made my get-a-way, the panicky feeling passed and I didn't know where to go. By the time I had visited several bars, I realized there was not going to be a massive hunt for me. I was ready to go back to the hospital. I hailed a police car and explained that I had wandered away from the mental hospital and he offered to drive me back. My absence was listed as an authorized leave and no disciplinary action was taken against me.

Some of the other patients experienced confusion and fits just as I did. Most of their fears and outbursts were based on imaginary incidents. One morning, during one of the group sessions, a woman who was there for killing her daughter, watched me intently. Her eyes bore through me like cold daggers. "Big Mary, do you want to discuss something with the group?" I asked.

"Devil eyes," she spat at me. "You have devil eyes, just like she did." With that she pounced at me with a knife she had stolen from the dining room. Dr. Stravenski yelled for me to run to the bath-room while she called for help. Big Mary was restrained immedi-ately but I was left with a feeling of helplessness. I realized how powerless a person was against the dangers that surrounded us. This realization increased my symptoms of depression. I started experiencing thoughts of suicide. I returned to my old habit of self-mutilation. My medication was increased.

I continued to fight the medication. I was determined not to be one of the people who sat around like vegetables day after day. Many sat around the lobby, never talking, never moving their own limbs or eyes.

The importance of taking our medication was constantly stressed. The staff used one of the patients as an example of what could happen if we quit taking our medication. The woman had been hospitalized for over twenty-five years for killing her mother. She was finally released and quit taking her medication. She was returned to the hospital, but not before she had killed her sister.

The patients came and went while the months for me stretched to a year and then another. I sent many letters to the California and Oregon Prisons asking to be allowed to transfer back to their institution. I explained that I now realized I was mentally ill and that I could control my behavior. The Superintendent for the women's prison in Oregon answered my letters but did not agree to take me back or help me transfer to another prison.

After I had been at St. Elizabeth for three years the Federal Government notified the hospital that my Federal sentence was almost over. Dr. Stravenski diagnosed my condition as "improved" and prepared my discharge papers. In support of her recommendation for discharge she cited my recent unauthorized leave from the movie, interpreting my actions as an indication that I was ready to enter society, but I realized that I was not prepared for any vocation. She recommended that I be returned to the prison in order to make a smoother transition back to society. She also interpreted my letters to the other prisons, requesting help in arranging a transfer, as acceptance of my mental disorder and with acceptance came cure. I was returned to Alderson to be processed out.

At Alderson, the stigma of having been in a mental hospital was evident. I was locked in an isolated cottage and kept heavily medicated. I was assigned a work detail in the dining room. The supervisor and other workers were afraid to work with me so I was assigned to work in an isolated food locker. No one was allowed in my area. If I had to come out of my area, I was treated like a dangerous animal. The depression, stemming from the fear of being ridiculed and feelings of inferiority, intensified by my surroundings and the heavy medication, produced new thoughts of death. I made several attempts at suicide. My medication would be increased and I would slip deeper into depression. I wrote several letters to Dr. Stravenski requesting that she insist that I be returned to the hospital. The Alderson staff soon joined me in my request to transfer me. After approximately four months I was returned to St. Elizabeth. St. Elizabeth housed me for another eight months. I was returned to Alderson to be processed out on my Federal charges and released to California for my state charges.

California housed me for another six months and gave me a discharge from all my sentences—all my fears and phobias went with me.

The following files accompanied my discharge;

September 10, 1968 Dr. Elizabeth R. Stravenski—Director Recommendation for Discharge

On admissions, the patient was on high doses of Thorazine as well as Mysoline. In spite of quite high doses of tranquilizing medication for nearly a year following admission, Miss Dortch remained quite tense and though non-psychotic, would appear periodically on verge of panic and on occasion would impulsively break window panes. Thereafter, she appeared more relaxed but still unable to discuss her feelings. Initially, she would refuse treatment for her wounds and though she gradually became more cooperative, would often remove the sutures shortly thereafter. During these periods, however, we were able to talk with her regarding her behavior as a gesture to deny her dependency and invite our rejection as she gradually became aware that she would not be secluded for this behavior the periods between gradually became longer. As the personnel came to know her better, increase in her anxiety could be noted and quite often was associated with whistling and she could be engaged in conversation and kept active and agree later that it was helpful. Her personality is that of an immature narcissistic individual who tries to use repression to keep her strong dependency needs from coming into awareness; however, this

94

mechanism at times breaks down and she then experiences extreme anxiety and tension. Of even more difficulty to help during her hospitalization was her marked dependency attachments to other patients and although disguised as lesbian aggressiveness, were more of a child-like seeking to do the mother's bidding. All too often in these relations when she could buy no more, she would be similarly rejected. In these incidents, she would often express rebellion, identifying her deprivation with authority and by remaining neutral and continuing to furnish her with assets or provide for her in the interim we have been able to somewhat work through this problem. She now has some sense of identity about her things and though she still tends to be over-generous with others, she is no longer the compulsive victim. As she became more able to experience some of her feelings of guilt and depression regarding her life situation and Elavile 25 milligrams four times daily was started with rather a good response and she has now been maintained on 25 milligrams three times daily. Very gradually her tranquilizers were reduced and she is currently well stabilized on Compazine 50 milligrams twice daily. Though the patient has never had any history of narcotic use during her periods of hospitalization, she has definitely tended to associate with patients with this problem. However, though she has on occasion been discovered with the apparatus, she had shown no changes in her own condition and it has been felt that this again is evidence of her being a compulsive victim and the ease with which she is influenced by others. Miss Dortch went on unauthorized leave from the movies on the hospital grounds on July 24, 1968, proceeded on foot, having several beers on the way before she was noticed by the Prince George County Police, to whom she explained her circumstances and who made arrangements for her return to the hospital by 1 a.m. Upon her return to the ward she was cooperative and though mildly intoxicated reacted as being rather childish and happy. When I saw her the next day, she expressed impulsive concern that her mother was ill and desired to go to her. She indicated that she soon realized she could not walk that far, had a few beers to relax herself, and was quite relieved when the police noticed her and could provide her return to the hospital. She seemed all too aware that she would revert to Class "A" and was almost too accepting of it, as if this episode were an example of her willingness, even though she lacks preparation for any sort of community adjustment. She realizes her need for vocational preparations and apparently is well motivated to return to prison and to pursue this, which is not available in our hospital security setting while serving sentence. She further indicates that she now feels she had a good relationship with the warden in Oregon substantiating this by pointing out that she was the one who realized that she was ill and arranged for hospitalization. She further indicates that there has been some correspondence between them and she feels this would give the basis for future understanding and the patient's continued progress. According to our Registrar's record, Miss Dortch will not be parole eligible or her sentence expire with good time until February, 1971. It is felt that she is well stabilized on her current medication, which is considerably less than she was receiving prior to hospitalization. It is, therefore, recommended that she be discharged to continue her sentence in a setting in which she could receive more vocational preparation than is possible in the security setting of a mental hospital.

December 27, 1968 Robert P. Hopkins
Consultant Psychiatrist

Miss Dortch was referred to me for evaluation about one month after her transfer from St. Elizabeth's Hospital because she was failing to adjust satisfactorily to Alderson. The major problem, as she reports it, in her adjustment was having to eat in the Central Dining Room with such a large number of people. She became increasingly restless and agitated and on her thirteenth day she smashed a window in the cottage and cut her wrist and so was admitted to the Hospital. She remained in the hospital for a few days and then was returned to the same program. About one week later, she reported to the Hospital stating that she felt agitated once again and requested admission. This request was acceded to. Two days after admission, while taking a shower, she discovered a razor blade which had been carelessly left behind by another resident. She took this razor blade and cut her arm superficially in several places. At the same time, she indicated verbally that she wished to be transferred back to St. Elizabeth and also wrote a letter to her doctor there. I have not seen her report from Elizabeth Hospital, but I believe that the diagnosis under the official classification would be schizoid personality (301.2). However, a more descriptive but unofficial diagnosis would be impulse-ridden character. The precise name of her diagnosis is less important than the functional disturbance. She presents two peculiar difficulties in the area of communication which

96

must be understood in order to effectively deal with her. The first problem which she exhibits, I conceptualize as a failure to believe in the effectiveness of verbal communication, thus when she has an intense feeling or an important message to communicate, she acts it out. The most recent example of this was her failure to report verbally her desire to be transferred back to St. Elizabeth and instead, the self-inflicting wounds with a razor blade which were intended to serve as a message indicating that she was very crazy and needed to be transferred. This is essentially an on-going game of charades which is, as anyone knows who has played, an inefficient and sometimes unreliable means of communication. The second problem which she displays in dealing with the people around her is that she does not communicate the same information to all the people who have contact with her. She does not lie and she doesn't contradict herself (usually), but she does communicate different bits of information to different persons such that they each gain a different picture of her. In dealing with a patient of this sort, it can not be over emphasized that all staff members having contact with her must communicate with all the others continuously. Failure to do so will result in the successful projection of the patient's compartmentalization and fragmentation on to the outside world so that her inner disorganization will be acted out by the hospital staff. Such a patient will require continuing vigilance for successful management for a very long period of time. This will of course require considerable staff time and effort.

January 3, 1969 Edith Jean Cooper, Staff Psychologist

Miss Dortch was referred for psychological evaluation because of the problem she has presented since her return here. On the Revised Beta Examination, Miss Dortch achieved an intelligence quotient of 166. This places her in the high range of intellectual functioning. Miss Dortch is characterized by chronic social maladjustment and the absence of pleasant experiences in her life. This includes feelings of abandonment by her family, feelings of having been victimized by other people, boredom, and feelings of alienation from her peers. Her social relationships are shallow. She has no strong ties to any other human being, in the adult sense of being able to give as much as she receives. Unpredictability is a prominent feature of her behavior. Miss Dortch is aggressive, dominating and competitive. She becomes threatened in situations which demand she behave in the socially-approved feminine way. This discomfort in her natural sex role is a component of the anxiety she experiences in groups and crowds; the presence of other people reminds her just how different she is. A more prominent component of Miss Dortch's anxiety in groups is her own awareness of how easily she gives in to her impulses. She is genuinely afraid of her own impulsive behavior because she knows she has not learned how to control it. An increase in the number of people in Miss Dortch's environment means an increase in the number of stimuli she experiences; an increase in the number of stimuli experiences means an increase in the probability that an impulsive behavior will be elicited. On direct questioning, she denied getting any satisfaction from knowing that other people are afraid of her, but she gave me some indirect indications that she finds others' fear very gratifying. She agreed with me that people don't keep on hurting themselves unless they get some satisfaction from doing so, but she wouldn't hazard a guess as to the particular satisfaction she gets. This is just as well, I think, because the admission that she uses chronic wrist-slashing to frighten and control others would be so threatening to Miss Dortch that it would disorganize her behavior almost completely. This knowledge about herself and her self-cutting behavior is, however, nibbling at the fringes of her awareness. Miss Dortch's behavior patterns are so well learned by now that eliminating them will be very difficult. Her MNPI protocol indicates little likelihood of significant personality change. She has achieved the only identity she has ever known, however unfortunate it may be, and will not easily relinquish it. It is my opinion that the patient requires intensive psychiatric treatment in a hospital equipped to deal with such patients. The hospital at the Federal Reformatory for Women in Alderson is not equipped to manage patients of this nature. This patient should be in a hospital where there are metal doors on the security rooms. Also there should be a locked security door leading to the area in which the security rooms are located. She should be on a unit where there is a male psychiatric aide on duty at all times. She should not be on a unit where a non-psychiatrically trained female nurse is on duty alone for sixteen out of every twenty-four hours. I believe it is possible to manage this patient medically at Alderson only in terms of the professional medical staff stationed here. However, it must be emphasized that Dr. Robert Hopkins is assigned as the NARA Director and serves the general population here only as a psychiatric consultant. Therefore he can-

not afford to devote a significant amount of time to the care and treatment of this patient. Also the time that this patient requires on the part of the General Medical Officers is very great because of the lack of other trained personnel. The medical doctors are the only segment of the staff at Alderson equipped to deal with this patient. The nurses and the rest of the hospital staff have not been trained in terms of handling seriously disturbed patients, and neither have the male or female correctional officers at this institution. It would not be advisable to rely on these non-trained individuals for assistance in treatment of this particular patient. Therefore, I recommend that this patient be transferred not to a penal institution, but to an all psychiatric treatment facility where appropriate psychiatric care and management can be given.

I flew to Little Rock and then took a bus to Russellville. Ruby and Sallyann met me at the bus station. Sallyann had tears in her eyes. It was the first time I had ever seen her cry.

Sallyann worked for Morton's Foods and was willing to help me get on at the plant where she worked. In the mean time I heard of a work program sponsored by the government. I put in an application and was among a group who were placed in a chicken processing plant near Russellville.

After two weeks of training, I became a floater, moving from job area to job area relieving other employees or doing temporary job assignments. I liked the work and there wasn't a job I couldn't handle.

On one occasion, I stayed over to help unload a truck. The men I worked with were surprised by my strength—I could lift as much as they could.

After a few weeks, I was called into the boss's office. "Come in, Miss Dortch," he said and motioned to a chair in front of his desk for me to sit down.

I moved to the chair, a premonition of doom washed over me as I sat facing this man.

He cleared his throat in an attempt at relieving the tension in the air. "It has been brought to my attention that you have only recently been released from prison," he stated. His words caused icy fingers to grip my heart. "I only ask this because one of the women who works here knows your mother and she saw you, on several occasions, cleaning your finger nails with a knife. She was very concerned for the safety of the other employees."

I couldn't look the man in the eyes. I stared at my shoes—they were splattered with chicken blood.

Again, he cleared his throat, "Is this true, Miss Dortch?"

"Yes," I answered in a coarse whisper. I was filled with shame and humiliation.

"Miss Dortch, why didn't you mention this on your application?" he asked, his tone pious.

I was now able to look at the man and I stared directly into his eyes. "Would you have hired me if I had told you?" I challenged him.

The man across the desk drew his eyes away from my cold stare and shuffled a stack of papers. "No," he admitted uncomfortably.

"That's why I didn't tell you. The chickens are in no danger of being stolen by me," I retorted, the sarcasm rising in my voice.

He ignored my comment. "Miss Dortch, I must ask you to resign, or pending an investigation we will have to terminate you."

I resigned and headed straight for the first bar. I needed a drink to forget the humiliation. The next few weeks were spent drinking. I added Preludes and LSD to my diet to cure my depression. I went from bar to bar, drinks and doing drugs.

I renewed my acquaintance with Bill, my homosexual friend from my teen years. Together we frequented the gay bars in near-by towns.

We left Russellville together. We shared a quiet camaraderie. I was comfortable with Bill. We both understood what it meant not be accepted. We traveled from city to city.

In a city somewhere—I can't remember where—a street prostitute approached me. I dressed mannish and she did not realize I was female.

"Hey Honey, do you want a good time?" she cooed seductively.

As I looked at her my anger intensified. "Yeah," I said. "Do you have something in mind?"

"Sure, Baby, your pleasure," she answered, eager for a trick.

I followed her to the motel around the corner and waited while she got the key to a room from the clerk. Her hands were on me immediately after closing the door. As soon as she realized that I was a woman she jumped back in disgust.

"How about that good time, Bitch," I snarled and grabbed the lamp that set near the bed and began hitting her in the head. Blood splattered the walls and bed but I kept beating her. Finally she lay in a bloody heap at my feet.

I dropped the lamp on her body and left the motel. I had no remorse or empathy for the woman I had just killed. I did not return to the motel for Bill but continued on my own journey of destruction from city to city, state to state—leaving a trail of violence behind me. The drugs and alcohol triggered the violence in me. The violence that was a part of my mental illness.

In a gay bar in Knoxville, Tennessee, I was sitting at the bar drinking, when a gay man approached me. He sat on the stool beside me and began a conversation. I didn't realize that he thought I was male until he placed his hand on my leg and moved it up to my groin.

"Surprise!" I announced when I saw his look of amazement.

He quickly walked away and joined a man at a table. Again the anger rose in me. The confusion I felt concerning my gender turned to anger—anger at others for not accepting me as I am. I watched the man for the rest of the evening and when he left the bar I followed him. When he got to his motel room I knocked on the door.

"Hi," I said with forced friendliness. "Remember me from the bar?"

"Oh sure, hey I'm sorry about how I acted. It was stupid," he apologized.

"Don't think anything about it. That's why I'm here. I thought you might have been given a jolt back there and I wanted to ease your mind."

"Hey, that's real nice of you," he said. "Want to come in for a drink?" he offered and moved back to let me into his motel room. I entered and looked around the room while he fixed us both a drink. As he handed it to me, I pulled out the .22 caliber revolver from my boot and held it against his head.

"Time to ease your mind," I said as I pressed the gun to his fore-

101

head and pulled the trigger. In the split second that it took to pull the trigger, I saw the terror and the realization that he was going to die rise to his eyes, but it didn't stop me. It was over in a moment and I left the motel.

As I walked down the street I began to hear the sound of sirens and I assumed someone had heard the gun shots and called the police. I walked faster, trying to put as much distance as possible between myself and the stranger in the motel room. When I heard the siren coming from behind me, I ducked in a telephone booth and picked up the receiver, pretending I was using it, in an effort at not being noticed by the police.

My efforts were in vain, however. The police car screeched to a stop and the two officers jumped out, their pistols drawn pointed at the telephone booth. "Come out, with your hands up," one of the officers ordered.

When I refused to come out, one of the officers held his gun on me while the other officer pulled me from the booth and threw me to the side walk. He placed his foot in the small of my back and snapped the handcuffs on me. I could taste the saltiness of my own blood from the cut on my lip. He quickly found the gun in my boot and stuck that in his own belt, then pulled me to my feet and shoved me in the back seat of the police car.

When we arrived at the jail, I was finger-printed and mug-shots were taken. One of the arresting officers loaded the typewriter with a form and began asking me questions. "What's you name and birth date?"

"Mary Dortch, three, twenty, forty-three," I answered.

"Sure it is...and my name is Little Red Riding Hood. Now give me your name and we can get on with this."

"That is my name...Mary Dortch," I assured him.

The officer sighed in exasperation and called to the other officer. "Johnny, see if we got anything on a Dortch on file, will you?"

I sat quietly while the officer, Johnny, checked the files. The officer typing the report tapped his pencil impatiently and glared at me with contempt. I met his stare with equal contempt.

"We have a Michael Dortch...rape...assault...robbery," the officer reported in a few minutes.

"That sounds like our man," the officer smirked and using two fingers, typed in the information.

"That's not me you dumb-ass," I tried to explain. "I told you my name is Mary Dortch."

The officer ignored my protest. "Birth date?" he asked.

"Why don't you just make that up too?" I snapped. The officer smiled and finished typing.

I was then taken to an interrogation room. Two detectives from homicide wanted information on the murder and several robberies that they were sure I was responsible for. I refused to answer any questions.

"Aren't you suppose to let me have an attorney present?" I asked.

"Can you afford an attorney?" one of the homicide detectives asked me.

"No, but I'm sure I don't have to answer any questions until I have an attorney with me."

"Well we aren't going to call you an attorney in the middle of the night."

"Then I'm not answering any questions." I replied.

One of the detectives motioned to the other and they left the room. I sat quietly for a few minutes but when they didn't return, I began to explore the room for a possible means of escape. There weren't any windows and I was sure the officers were right outside the only door. I checked the coats on the coat rack for keys. When my hand felt something hard, I flipped the coat back to see what was under it. An officer had hung his police revolver and holster on the coat rack and covered it with his coat. My hands moved to the gun but froze mid-way. I was sure the gun was left there on purpose for me to find. If I tried to escape then I would be shot down. I covered the revolver and holster back up with the coat and returned to my chair.

A few minutes later the detectives returned. I watched their faces as they entered. Their eyes moved to the coat rack and I was sure my suspicions had been correct.

The detectives did not question me any further but I was taken to the line-up room. There I stood with five men while an elderly woman swore that I was the 'man' she had seen committing the robbery of a motel.

"Okay, that's all...Let's go," one of the arresting officers said and walked to the line up and took me by the arm. I was escorted down a long corridor made of gray block. The officer opened two doors made of steel bars with a brass key from the key-ring at his belt.

"Here we go, Home-Sweet-Home," he said as he began to open another door.

I stared in horror at the eight or nine men who occupied the cell this officer was going to place me in. "Oh no, you aren't going to put me in with those damn men. I told you I'm a woman."

The officer's eyes traveled down my body. "Well we ain't going to put you in with the women," he informed me in a sarcastic tone.

"Then you had better damn well put me in the drunk tank or some other single cell because I'm not going in with those men."

The officer's eyes narrowed. "Are you sure that you ain't a man...I can find out for sure, you know?"

"You had better not try strip searching me...not unless you have a matron on duty." I retorted.

The officer took three long strides to a room marked, Dispatcher, and called. "Connie."

A bleached blond woman appeared and the two whispered together. The blond shook her head several times and I could tell she was refusing to strip search me.

The officer turned to me and motioned "Come on, we'll put you in the juvenile cell until morning. They can decide then what they will do with you."

I stayed in the single cell until morning when two officers arrived and I was taken to a nearby county and housed for thirty days. No one explained any reason for my move but I suspected that the reason was the confusion in my gender. In four weeks I was returned and I saw an attorney for the first time, ten minutes before I was to go on trial. My attorney advised me to plead guilty and I was sentenced to five life sentences for the murder and several robberies in the area.

When Ruby and Mama heard what had happened they were

sure that Bill had been the one who had killed the man. It eased my conscience for them to think that it was Bill and when a year later, Bill committed suicide, they were sure that he was full of remorse for letting me go to prison for his crime. I knew Bill's reason for taking his own life was he could not stand living any longer in a society that couldn't accept him—a society that thought homosexuality was a mental disorder or that gay people were freaks. He was tired of trying to fit into a society that didn't want him.

CHAPTER 9

Tennessee Prison for Women—1971 to 1979

A male correctional officer, Sergeant Dison, and a female correctional officer, Officer Ridder, from Tennessee Prison for Women traveled the three hundred fifty miles to Knoxville to transport me to the women's prison. I sat in the back of the cruiser and the two officers sat in the front. Strips of metal were welded together to form a latticed divider but still allowed conversation. Dison was an elderly man with snow white hair. He was built thin and stood over six feet. He talked with the slow drawl of the South.

"The sheriff told me you created a little ruckus for them," Dison told me.

"I didn't create anything...except that I wouldn't let them put me in the cell with the men."

"Yeah...yeah, that's what he said," Dison laughed.

I didn't see anything amusing.

"You do look like a teen-age boy, you know," he continued.

"Well, I can't help that," I said, my voice full of sarcasm.

"How long have you had those chin whiskers?" Dison asked.

"A couple of years, is it a problem with you?"

"Nope...no problem with me...most women would pluck them out."

"Well, I'm not most women," I said, resenting his frankness. The truth of the matter was that I was proud of the chin whiskers.

"Yeah...yeah, you're a real bad ass. Did you know that you had been scheduled to be transported to Petrose, the men's prison?" Dison asked, proud of the effect his words had on me. I had not been aware of any such thing but I was not going to give this man the satisfaction of knowing that I was surprised.

106

"Yeah," Dison continued in a long drawl. "All ready to go to the men's prison and then the very day you were to go, your FBI sheet arrived in the mail. Your finger prints proved you really were who you said you were...Mary Catherine Dortch. What did you kill that fellow for?"

"Because he asked me too many questions," I said, glaring at Dison.

He understood my meaning and was not intimidated.

"Yeah...yeah, a real bad ass," he repeated shaking his head.

He picked up my folder from the seat and began to read it while the female officer drove in silence. I watched his face as he read. His eyebrows raised several times. When he was finished, a silence hung over us like a dark cloud. I could sense the uneasiness in this man.

"This prison isn't so bad," Dison began in an effort at continuing a conversation. "Dorothy Greer is the warden over at the women's prison. She hasn't been warden long but she is all right. We had a riot a few months ago and the big bosses thought that the other warden needed to be replaced. There aren't but about sixty-five women in the prison. Pretty small compared to the California prison you were in, huh?"

When I didn't make any comment, Dison continued, "Yeah...It's a much smaller institution then what you've been in and I bet you'll see that the rules are not as rigid as the institutions where you've been incarcerated in the past. The staff uses their own judgment as to enforcing discipline or creating rules to abide by. There's never been a need to enforce strict security. Most of the staff rule with compassion."

Dison continued his description of the institution for most of the trip. Before we reached Nashville, we had to zigzag to Chattanooga to pick up another female prisoner to be transported to the women's prison.

Dison stayed with me in the cruiser, while the female officer went in the county jail to do the paper work on the other prisoner. I remained in the back seat while Dison got out to stretch his legs and smoke. While he was leaning against the car, a sheriff's deputy walked by.

"Hey Dison, how you doing?" the deputy called.

"As little as possible," Dison called back.

The deputy looked in my direction. "I thought you didn't transport men," the deputy queried.

"I don't," Dison replied without further explanation or comment on my appearance.

The deputy joined Dison and the two men continued on in conversation about other topics. A bit later, a county cruiser pulled into the parking lot and two arresting officers helped a man 'dressed in drag' from the back seat and escorted him up the steps to the jail.

"Humph," Dison snorted. "It looks to me that you have some strange ones yourself."

The other female prisoner and the correctional officer arrived and we were soon on our way to Nashville.

When I arrived at the prison, I was locked in a dorm cell. I could see Sergeant Dison from my wicket talking with the dorm officer. As he talked, the officer would look in my direction. I remembered him reading my files and suspected he was filling the officer in on my past history.

I remained locked down for the next four days. I wasn't allowed out even to bathe. I received the usual kites from other inmates telling me about the institution. I learned that inmates are not usually locked down when they arrive. When the officer brought me my food, I questioned her about being locked down without being allowed to bathe.

"That's our orders," she answered without adding any explanation.

"But for how long?" I continued.

"Until Corporal Harris returns and can order different."

"I don't think they meant that I couldn't be let out to shower," I tried to reason with the officer.

"I'm sorry, Sergeant Dison said you were to be locked down until Corporal Harris came back. He didn't mention letting you out to shower or anything."

"Well, can't you ask Sergeant Dison?" I asked, my voice full of the impatience I felt.

"He's off. We can't call him at home unless it's an emergency."

I gave up my efforts and decided to wait for Corporal Harris. These officers were as programmed to obey authority as Hitler's army, I thought.

The cell that I was in had a single bed, made of blond wood, and matching chest of drawers. There was also a metal locker for hanging clothes and a regular sink and commode. It also had a large window which cranked out. No bars were utilized. I could see the grounds and they resembled a college campus. Sidewalks connected the different buildings. The grass was well maintained with shrubs and flowers.

The fence that surrounded the institution was approximately eight feet high. No razor wire was used across the top. I learned through the kite system that no perimeter control was utilized as there was a very low escape rate.

Four days later, Corporal Helen Harris, the dorm's commanding officer returned to work from vacation and ordered me to be released and permitted me to shower. I was released into population and was assigned a job of cleaning light fixtures.

Two days after I was released into population, I was in the day area. Several card tables were scattered around one end of the room and a television occupied the other end. A glass wall divided the two areas. I was suddenly overcome by a blinding panic. I felt the familiar surge of fear in my stomach. Then I got a dreadful mental picture of everyone looking at me, laughing at me because I was crazy. Had I been in control of my wits I would have noticed that only a few women occupied the day area and their attentions were occupied elsewhere, but in my mind there were hundreds of women in the room and they were all staring at me. My fear turned to rage. If they thought I was crazy, I would show them crazy. I began to hit the glass room-divider with my fist. The blood spurted from my hand, soaking my clothes. I was immediately restrained and put in the dry cell while medical was called. These cells were windowless and the only fixtures were a seatless toilet and stainless steel sink. A metal cot was anchored to the floor. The metal door contained a wicket. These cells were used in cases where an inmate was on a suicide watch or extremely violent.

In the dry cell, I began to get a hold of myself. It was so quiet in the cell. The only sound was that of my own frightened breathing. The cell had a tomb-like atmosphere. I began to relax. A wave of peace washed over me. I wanted the peace to go on forever. I craved the peace of death.

I took a t-shirt and tied it tightly around my neck. My neck began to swell from the restriction, making me unable to breath. Corporal Harris heard the light thud of my body hitting the floor as I lost consciousness. As my body began to twitch in convulsions, my feet hit the metal door in an eerie-rhythmic sound of a heart beat, causing her blood to chill. She rushed into my cell and with a pair of scissors, proceeded to cut the material of the t-shirt tied around my neck.

I could hear the sound of her voice calling to me. "You're going to be all right...breathe...you'll be all right...nothing is so bad that this is the answer...breathe."

The medical staff arrived; I was given oxygen, and the cuts on my arms were attended to.

I was placed on a suicide watch and confined to the dry cell for my own protection. I remained in the dry cell for several months and was put on large doses of Thorazine. The doses of Thorazine increased my depression. I did not want to take the medication. I felt that the medication was the root of my unexplained fears and sudden burst of violence.

During one of the visits to the doctor, I sat on the examining table in his sterile room, pleading to discontinue my medication. The doctor stood at my feet. He had thin, dull gray hair. He wore a white knee-length lab coat that did little to camouflage his shoulders set in a permanent slouch. A stethoscope dangled around his neck. His eyes were bored behind black Buddy Holly-type glasses.

"Please don't make me take the medicine. It's driving me crazy...the medication is what causes me to act crazy. I am not crazy...the medication causes me to lose control," I tried to explain.

"Now, Mary, I think you are being a little melodramatic. This medication is for your own good. It may take a while for you to adjust to it. Let's give it a few weeks and if you don't see a change, then we will change the medication," the doctor insisted.

I resented the use of the name Mary—even though it was my

110

given name. I resented not being allowed to decide for myself if I should take the medication or not. I felt trapped and frightened. The doctor handed me the paper cup which contained the brown Thorazine tablets. I felt the familiar rage rise in me.

I slapped the medication from the doctor's hands, causing the tablets to sail through the air and land on the floor across the room. I leapt off the table and grabbed the doctor as he was turning to flee from the room. He began to shout, and seconds later, I was blinded by a searing hot pain. My face felt as if hot grease had been thrown in it. I released the doctor to protect myself from the consuming pain. I could hear the faint hiss of the mace can as the doctor continued to spray its contents at me.

My screams of pain echoed down the corridor then my arms were jerked away from my face and pinned behind my back. I could feel the handcuffs being snapped around my wrist. My face continued to burn in unbearable pain as I was shoved toward the dry cell and pushed in.

"When we take the handcuffs off, you will be able to wash you face in the sink," the officer said to me.

When the handcuffs were removed, I stumbled towards the sink. I ran my hands frantically across the wall above the sink, searching for the button that would turn on the water. It required continuous pressure on the button. The sink was designed to prevent flooding of the cells by inmates. When I had found it, I pressed the button with a thumb of one hand and splashed cold water with the other hand. The process did little to relieve my pain.

After several minutes, I was able to open my eyes. I grabbed a match stick and jammed it in the button to cause to button to lock in place. I then stuffed a washcloth in the drain to catch water in the sink. I was then able to use both hands to splash cold water on my face. In about thirty minutes the pain eased. I examined my face in the foggy metal mirror above the sink. My eyes were swollen to tiny slits in my face. My skin was red and blistered. The skin was too tender to blot dry so I left my face wet and lay down on the cot. I had never felt so much pain in my life. I lay there for most of the night. I would doze off only to be awakened by the pain. I splashed water on my face several times during the night. By morning, the

111

pain had eased but the swelling was still there. This lasted for three days.

Mace was used frequently on me after that time. If I refused the medication, I was maced. If I showed any signs of violence, I was maced. The staff was trained to believe that mace was a method to gain control of a violent situation without physical damage. The terror that some staff members had of me caused them to panic and use the mace frequently.

On another occasion, when I refused the medicine, it was ordered to be administered intravenously. Don Farrar, who was the Assistant Warden of Administration, and Sergeant Dison entered my cell to restrain me so that the nurse could give me the shot. As Farrar entered the cell I grabbed him by his tie. Dison had predicted my action and had the can of mace already to spray. When I jumped back from the searing pain, Farrar's tie, that I still had in my hand came with me. I immediately felt the prick of the needle in my arm. Despite the pain I was still confused with the piece of material that I held in my hand like a limp snake. Had I grabbed the man so strongly that I had actually ripped off his tie? The dilemma was quickly put to the back of my mind as I stumbled to the sink to splash the cold water on my face. While I was occupied with easing the burning pain, I heard the cell door being re-opened and someone hurrying in. I sensed, rather than saw—because my eyes were swollen shut—someone searching for something on the floor and then hurrying out.

Later Dison explained to me what had happened. "When you grabbed Farrar, his damn clip-on-tie came off. That was him trying to get his tie back," he laughed.

"Clip-on-tie?" I asked. "What's a clip-on-tie?"

"Oh, they make a tie that you don't have to be bothered with tying. All the young dandies use them now," Dison sniffed. Despite the seriousness of the situation, I was able to find it funny and we both laughed at the incident.

Dison was able to make me see some humor in the horror I was experiencing. I think now that it was an attempt at helping me keep my sanity—a means of keeping a grip on reality.

The drugs continued to be administered to me to keep me in

control—sometimes in such massive dosages it endangered my life. Most thought of me as an animal and treated me that way. Their cruel treatment only added to the nightmare that I felt would never end. Sometimes the isolation, and horrors conjured up from the medication became unbearable; I would explode into fits of violence. The violence only resulted in the guards being terrified of me. The terror that I could instill in the staff was my only revenge for the nightmare I was living.

I enjoyed their terror and sought every opportunity to add to it. Most of my escapades were done during the thirty minute exercise periods. I would spend the time alone in the dry cell, plotting how to terrorize the staff. Some things were harmless—like the time I spent days unscrewing the eight screws that held the metal mirror to the block wall in the dry cell. When I had succeeded in taking the mirror off, I spread it out for the staff to see what I had done.

On several occasions, I was able to get out of handcuffs or in some instances, I was able to break the handcuffs. Other times, I would go for long periods without eating.

There was no disciplining me—I wasn't afraid of anything. I was totally insensitive to any punishment.

Some staff members who were afraid of me used the medication to keep me sedated. There was no control on the amount of drugs administered. It was administered as needed. Many times the staff would administer it until I went to sleep. On one occasion, I was given shots every forty-five minutes. My blood pressure dropped to a drastic 90/30.

I became more and more withdrawn. My only show of emotion was the frequent hysterical outbursts. I refused to talk with the staff psychologist. I resented his prying.

I continued to stay locked down. The prison added a steel door in the middle of one dormitory hall to divide ten rooms off for a segregation unit. The purpose of these rooms was to place inmates in isolation for punishment. Many times after a violent outburst, I would be placed in one of these rooms. I would be the only inmate in this area as much as eight or nine months at a time.

Warden Greer left the administration three months after I arrived and Penny Bernhardt was hired to fill her position. She was a tall slim woman, with dark hair. She was very compassionate and made herself available to the inmates to discuss problems. She believed in rehabilitation as an alternative to punishment, but I was a constant concern for her. On several occasions she attempted some form of therapy. On one occasion she allowed a volunteer church woman to provide me with a canvas and acrylic paints. I really wasn't interested in the art supplies but I did paint a crude painting of a bunch of flowers for the church lady, and used some of the remaining paints to make bright patterns on art paper. Warden Bernhardt visited my cell often and would stand at my door with the wicket open. She would balance an ash tray on the open wicket door while we talked. She always had praise for me, and I enjoyed her praise. I showed her my designs and she selected several to hang in her office.

"I have always been interested in Van Gogh," I told her. "Not so much his art as his life. I always understood his heartache at not being accepted by society."

"Yes," Ms. Bernhardt agreed, "I am sure he did live a very lonely life."

"Have you ever heard the song *Starry Starry Night'*?" I asked her, "It's a song about his life. It brings tears to my eyes whenever I hear it."

"Yes, I've heard it. It is a beautiful song." Warden Bernhardt agreed.

Many times while I was in segregation, Ms. Bernhardt or Sergeant Dison would be the only people I would talk with for weeks at a time. The staff that had to check on me or bring me my meals would complete their task and hurry away. Sergeant Dison was concerned about my extended isolation and asked that he be allowed to take me out with him. Ms. Bernhardt arranged for him to take me—on a trial basis—for thirty minutes a day. Gradually the time was increased. Ms. Bernhardt later gave him permission to let me out to mow the yard or work in the guard station. He was the only person who was allowed to take me out and he was always there to supervise me. Sometimes he would take me to lunch in the prison's cafeteria. I would have to sit with him at the table, along with the other male officers. At the time women officers did not carry mace and were not qualified to shoot guns.

A few months after Dison began taking me out with him, he told me about his promotion. "Well, in a few days I'll be wearing captain's bars," he boasted.

"That's great. How did you manage that?" I asked.

"Well...this young officer who used to work here, wanted to go with the ball team to play the free world folks. I thought he was sweet on one of the women and wouldn't let him go. The day of the game he called in sick and went over to the park where the game was. So I fired his ass. I told them down front not to let him back on the compound. He came anyway and went down to the sergeant's shack. He wanted to get up in my face and tell me that I didn't have the authority to fire him because I was just a sergeant. I gave him a dose of what we sometimes have to do to you...I maced him. The little bastard swore out a warrant against me for assault. They came out to the house to arrest me. But when they found out I worked for the state, they dropped the charges. The next day I told Miss Penny that I needed captain's bars and she said 'done.'"

I laughed. I liked Dison's arrogance.

Captain Dison and I would have long talks. He understood my mental problems but was not intimidated by them. He also realized that much of my foolishness was to mess with the staff's heads. I grew to respect him and he became a father figure to me.

Dison had asked me several times why I had killed the man in Knoxville. I refused to tell him. He had read the facts of the case and had his own theory. Apparently the stranger had been living with a teen-age boy. He thought the boy had really killed the man and I had felt that my life was already so messed up that I had taken the rap. I let him think whatever he wanted.

Captain Dison occasionally would give me magazines to read. I was especially interested in history and war. From one of the magazines I clipped a coupon to have your family history traced. When the literature arrived, it explained briefly the history of the name Dortch. It was a German name and its original spelling was D-e-u-t-s-c-h-e.

This triggered a fascination with my German heritage. I used a scrap of cloth to make an arm band and drew a swastika emblem on it. I also shaved my head and during the exercise periods I would do the goose-step around the lobby, stopping periodically to do the salute of Hitler's army and shout "Heil Hitler."

Captain Dison was not pleased. He took my arm band away from me and gave me a firm lecture. "Lee, most of the time when you act like a nutty-buddy, I think it's funny. I know you are just doing it to get attention, but you have gone too far with this. It isn't funny."

I hadn't realized that men of his age had experienced Hitler's cruelty first hand.

Dison might have thought my behavior was funny but he was also aware of the seriousness of my mental problems. On one occasion he told me he had recommended Central State Mental Institution but they wouldn't take me.

"See, I told you I wasn't insane." I beamed.

"No, that isn't it." He shook his head sadly. "They say you are too mentally ill for them to handle. You only have brief periods of violence, they have no way of monitoring you. They are afraid of you—they can't risk taking you. The only way they will accept you is if you go off the deep end and stay. It's sad for you, but that's the way it is."

Dison was firm with me on all occasions. He knew how easily I could manipulate a situation to my advantage. As long as I played by his rules he arranged for me to have privileges, but if he felt that my behavior warranted discipline, then he was quick to enforce it—including mace and isolation.

"Why do you hate me?" I asked him one day.

He handed me a cigarette. "I don't hate you," he said and sat down beside me.

"Why do you mace me so much if you don't hate me?" I asked innocently.

"Consider the circumstances," he said. "There is no control over you. I can't strike you. Mace does the least harm."

"I would rather be hit," I cried.

"Yeah, I know, but mace doesn't do any permanent damage, and we have to use it. I can't hit you, plus getting close to you when you are like that is dangerous. Right now you are a different

116

person. You are intelligent and easy to talk with—you have a variety of knowledge." He smiled.

Captain Dison had a dry way of viewing life. When a university doctor who was doing a paper on homosexuality asked him to interview some of the true homosexuals in the institution, Dison told him that he only knew of one. He gave him my name and the doctor set up an interview with me. I was asked a series of questions, and he ran a blood test to determine if my homosexuality was hereditary, a hormone imbalance, or a result of my environment. The doctor was interested in my bone structure, pointing out that my hands were small men's hands and that my forehead was more masculine shaped. He tested my strength and determined that I was excessively strong for a woman. When his research was concluded, he determined that I had a hormone imbalance.

"Humph," Captain Dison sniffed. "You don't need Ph.D. to know you have a hormone imbalance. You can just look at that damn beard you've sprouted to know that."

The doctor's diagnosis, from charting my facial and other bone structure, was that I was a transsexual—that I was male in a female body. This diagnosis triggered a battery of requests from me to the warden for a sex-change operation. I was certain that the doctor's diagnosis was correct. I approached her with my request on every occasion that she was present when Captain Dison had me in the dining room.

Her face would turn scarlet and she would assure me that she would check into it.

After several requests, she announced that she had made the decision and that she would arrange for my sex-change operation and my transfer to the Walls, which was the men's prison.

"The Walls...," I cried. "I don't want to go to the men's prison."

"Oh, you will have to," she explained. "Once you have the operation, you will be a male. You will no longer be able to be housed here at the women's prison."

This was not in my plans. I returned to Captain Dison's table full of concern. "I don't want to go to the men's prison," I told him sadly.

"You damn fool," he growled. "I told her to tell you all that bull

117

shit to shut you up about that damn sex-change operation."

I breathed a sigh of relief and never mentioned a sex-change operation again.

In 1973, my mother became ill. She wasn't expected to live much longer. The shock was devastating. A life-time of guilt for the sorrow that I had caused her crashed around my head. My only desire was to escape...escape from prison...escape from the hurt and guilt.

My chance came one day as I as leaving medical. As I passed by the door leading to Central Control, I noticed that it was made in such a fashion that the bottom could be closed and the top could swing back. Someone had left the top door open. I reached my hand across the top of the door and unlocked the bottom half. I had a shank in my sock that I had made from a pair of scissors another inmate had given me. I quickly pulled it out. As I entered Central Control, I grabbed Officer Osborne, a pretty young black officer in her twenties, and held the shank to her throat. Her body was stiff from fear and I practically had to drag her towards the door leading to the parking lot.

"Let's go...we'll drive your car," I ordered. Officer Long was an older black officer who had worked at the institution much longer than Officer Osborne. She had not made any attempt at calling for assistance. She noted the fear in the young officer's face and stepped forward.

"I'll go with you, Lee...take me," she offered.

I blinked in surprise. "I don't care which of you go with me but one of you will."

Officer Long grabbed her purse and moved in my direction. I released Officer Osborne, pushing her towards the desk and Officer Long moved towards me.

"Don't let anyone through here, if you want to see your friend again." I ordered and ushered Officer Long out the door.

"My car is over here," Long said and pointed in the direction of a compact car. We hurried to it and were on our way in seconds.

Tennessee is full of hills and streams and I was not familiar with the area. Officer Long drove in the direction that I indicated without any further comment. We drove for what seemed like an eternity on back roads that didn't lead anywhere.

My journey stopped when we came to a river which required crossing a ferry to get to the other bank. Some instinct warned me that if I attempted to cross the river on the ferry the police could radio the boat. I did not want to be stranded in the middle of the river and chose to turn back. Officer Long was able to turn the small car in the middle of the road and we returned the way we had just come. We had driven less then a mile when we ran into a road block.

"Damn...can you break through?" I yelled.

"Not in this small car," the officer explained reasonably. I realized she was right. To ram the patrol cars blocking the road would be sure death. The small car was surrounded immediately. The police officers ordered us out of the car and both of us to lie face down while they put the handcuffs on us.

"I'm the officer," Long protested.

"We can't take the chance," the policeman explained as he put both of us in the back of the patrol car. I was later to learn that the prison had not released a description of me. This negligence saved my life, the police had to treat us both with caution for without a description, they couldn't shoot the one in the prison uniform for fear we may have exchanged clothes.

The newspapers had a field day with my escape. The warden explained that I was under psychiatric treatment and received constant medication.

I was returned to the prison and locked back into segregation. When my mother died, the chaplain refused to deliver the message. Captain Dison was off so the chaplain waited two days until Dison returned to have him deliver the message. I vowed then, that I wanted no part of that man's Christian teaching.

"You wouldn't have pulled a fool stunt like that if I had been on duty," Dison growled at me later. "I've told those damn women, time and time again, to keep that door locked. They are more interested in looking good then keeping prisoners from escaping. Hell, Lee, why didn't you take the pretty one when you left?" Dison asked in his usual dry manner.

"The other one said she wanted to go. I didn't care which one went."

"Well, Officer Osborne wouldn't let anyone out of the prison because she was afraid you would kill Long. They had a devil of a time trying to get out to go after you. They had to break the sally port open to get out to notify someone you had escaped."

"I told her not to let anyone out," I admitted.

"Well, she sure as hell obeyed your orders." Dison sniffed.

At my first review to determine if I should be allowed out of segregation, the administration agreed that it didn't ever intend to release me into inmate population. The medication continued to be administered on a regular basis without the supervision of a doctor. The medication continued to cause phobias and violence without warning. Another outburst of violence erupted during one of the exercise periods. I had a habit of using this time to read an article from the newspaper called *Love Is*. I asked an inmate—a new inmate who was unfamiliar with my violence—for the section of the newspaper.

"No you can't have it," she snapped.

As I walked off, I heard her laugh and say "That crazy son of a bitch won't get this *Love Is*."

I returned to my cell but the hurt and embarrassment this woman had caused me ignited my anger. I interpreted the curse "that son of a bitch" as an insult to my mother, so I felt justified when I left the cell, went to the laundry room and grabbed a mop that had a metal handle.

Before anyone could stop me, I walked to the table where the woman was sitting. Raising the steel mop handle high above her head, I brought it down with such force that I could hear her head crack like a watermelon. Blood spilled over the table and her clothes. I raised the mop handle again for a second blow when someone touched me on the arm.

"Don't hit her again...she is dead, baby...don't hit her again."

I looked in the direction of the soft voice. Linda Ferris, a young black inmate, stood reaching for the weapon, unconcerned for her own safety. I handed the mop handle to her.

"That's good," she continued to speak soothingly. "That's good...go sit down baby...maybe when the officers get here they

120

won't mace you if you are calm," she added.

I looked around. There were no officers in sight. I went to the sofa in the lobby to wait while Linda hid the mop handle.

When security arrived, they demanded the mop handle and threatened to lock Linda down if she didn't produce it. She remained silent.

"Give it to them, Linda. It's not worth it." I instructed.

She retrieved the mop handle from where she had hidden it and gave it to the officers. The woman lived and I stayed in segregation for nine months, then returned to my cell in the dorm but I was still locked down. In every yearly review hearing it was always agreed that I would never be released into population, so I remained locked in my cell unless I showed any signs of violence, then I would be moved to segregation. If I showed any signs of depression or the staff thought that I was suicidal, I would be moved to the dry cell. My meals were served on paper plates or plastic trays without any eating utensils. I was to eat my meals like an animal. On one occasion, I threw the tray in Officer M.B. Smith's face.

Occasionally an officer would show kindness and I was treated with compassion. I craved the compassion and returned it willingly—eager to please.

Officer Deak, a new officer, brought me my breakfast one morning. When she looked at the pancakes—with butter and syrup—her face expressed the empathy she held for having to feed me without benefit of a fork.

I met her eyes with understanding and reached for my tray and began to eat calmly, pinching off bits of the sticky pancake with my fingers and putting it in my mouth.

"Why didn't you hit me with the tray?" she asked.

"The other officer treated me like an animal; I acted like an animal. You, on the other hand, treated me with respect. You showed remorse for not being allowed to give me a fork. I respect you for that," I explained.

Officer Deak was a short woman with reddish hair and a smile for everyone. She had a bubbly personality and a cute southern accent. In her spare time she sang with a country-western band. She would talk with me about her dreams of being a singer. She was a religious person and always treated me fairly. I returned the fair treatment.

On an occasion when the warden had visited my cell, she left a metal ashtray sitting on the wicket door. She remembered it when she returned to her office and called back to the officer's desk to have them retrieve it. But she was too late. I had already flattened and hidden it.

The officers searched the cell thoroughly. When their search proved fruitless, I was handcuffed and escorted to medical where I was stripped searched. Still no ashtray was found.

I was returned to my cell and spent the next few days bending the flattened ashtray and sharpening it on the concrete floor to make a shank.

I knew the officers were not allowed to open the cell without two officers being available so I would wait until an officer was alone and call her to my wicket. When I held up the shank, she would rush back to the desk to call for assistance but I would have hidden the shank before the another officer arrived. My cell would be searched but the shank couldn't be found. I would then be taken to medical and stripped searched again. This went on for several days.

My smoking privileges were taken away until I agreed to give them the shank but I still held out. Officer Deak finally pleaded with me. "Lee, give me the shank so they will let you smoke."

"Okay," I answered. "Turn your back."

She turned her back and I fished the homemade knife from the hole in the wall around the plumbing and handed it to her.

"Why didn't you give it to the officer earlier?" she asked.

"No one asked me to," I answered smugly.

Officer Falk was another officer who showed compassion. Many times I would refuse to eat unless they would give me a utensil to eat with. On one occasion I had gone twenty-nine days without eating. Officer Falk was working the midnight shift. She had brought a box of Cheerios to eat. I watched her through the wicket as she sat munching the dry cereal and milk. Cheerios was not something you could get inside the penitentiary and I had loved them as a child.

"I may be persuaded to eat a bit of those Cheerios," I called to her.

She smiled knowingly and handed me a bowl of them. I devoured the bowl of cereal in minutes.

Officer Falk never showed any signs of fear toward me. We spent a lot of time talking through the wicket. She proved her trust one evening when a piece of food became lodged in her throat. She moved to my wicket where I could reach her to hit her on the back to dislodge the food. Her keys were within reach but I didn't breach her trust.

Another time she was on crutches. It was required that she had to come to work. When she attempted to open another inmate's wicket she lost her balance. I reached through my wicket and caught her. She was never afraid that I would reach for her keys.

I was persistent in anything I chose to accomplish. Once I spent weeks digging through the block wall with a piece of metal that I broke off the plumbing under the sink. I was sure my plan was a secret. I didn't realize that the continuous pecking on the blocks was being monitored by the staff. When I was taken out for exercise my progress was checked.

Officer Falk was on duty when the pecking sound changed in tone. She was sure that I was near breaking through the outer wall and called security.

The newspaper and television crew were always eager for a story concerning me, so while Officer Falk waited for security and the television crew she assumed would be there she applied fresh make-up. Her efforts at looking nice for the television camera were all in vain—no one showed up.

When I was taken out to exercise the next day, still unaware that my plan was known, my personal belongings were moved to another cell. All the weeks of digging had been in vain.

I was to spend a total of nine years in isolation. Six of those years were spent in the dry cell. In the regular isolated cell I could see outside my window, and staff and some inmates were allowed to talk with me through the wicket. Sometimes the isolation would cause deep depression and I would try to take my life by cutting my arms. I would then be moved to the dry cell for protection—to

123

protect me from myself.

The long periods of time that I spent in the dry cell began to cause sensory deprivation. Scientists have tested the effects of sight, sound and touch deprivation, only to have the subject of the experiment become hysterical, or experience hallucinations in a short period. The human mind cannot be totally deprived of sight and sound. It will create its own sight and sound if none is present.

I began to hear voices in the cell with me. I believed them to be demons trying to communicate with me. When I mentioned it to Dr. Tregel, the consulting psychologist, he ordered that I be allowed at least four books a week to read and access to religious material.

I would read the books in the first few days of the week. When I ran out of books to read I would read and re-read the Bible. I was especially interested in the Book of Revelations. Few ministers preach from this book because it is so open for interpretation. I was still sure that the voices I heard were not my imagination and were the voices of the devil and that I was chosen to be one of his disciples. Chapter Thirteen, verse eighteen of the Book of Revelations stated:

Here is wisdom. Let him that have understanding count the number of the beast; for it is the number of man; and his number is six hundred three score.

With the realization that verse eighteen was a set of three sixes, I believed I had solved the first enigma, and searched the Bible for more clues to the message I was to receive.

I compared Chapter Twelve, verse fifteen with my own experience of being carried away during a flood when I was a child.

And the serpent cast out of his mouth as a flood after a woman. And he might cause her to be carried away in a flood.

I was born in March. My zodiac sign is Pisces, the fish, so all reference to the sea was compared to my being a fish.

...and the beast shall rise up out of the sea, having seven heads...

The silence of the dry cell was compared to Chapter Eight.

And when he had opened the seventh seal, there was a silence in heaven.

The reference to the number seven in these verses and other

124

verses was compared with my prison number which ended in three sevens.

...and he causeth...to receive a mark in their right hand, or in their forehead

The Spanish time mark that Anna had tattooed on my forehead was my mark of the beast. To be extra sure that I was marked for the beast, I tattooed a serpent in the palm of my hand. I used a needle that another inmate sent me in a kite, and also, ground-up pencil lead.

This verse explained my masculine bone structure and facial hair which was in direct conflict with my naturally curly hair—combination of feminine and masculine features. It further explained my confusion with my gender.

...and their faces were faces of men...and they had hair of women.

I believed if I proved to be a loyal disciple I would be given power. I practiced my powers daily. I would lay a piece of paper on the end of my cot and sit for hours willing it to levitate. I would try different distances to test my power—moving closer to the paper with the belief that my power had not developed enough to levitate the paper from a distance. Occasionally, the wind from my breath would flutter the paper slightly. I would be ecstatic—sure that my powers were soon coming. I was sure that all I needed was to prove myself worthy as the devil's disciple.

...and power was given to him...

This, to me, meant I should have no conscience or show signs of remorse or acts of compassion. I should not have any emotional bonds. I began to train myself to become without a conscience. I would hurl cruel insults to the staff members and make malicious threats. I discontinued all correspondence with my family and destroyed all pictures of Mama, Ruby and Sallyann. I would try to envision doing them harm, to test my lack of conscience, but my affection would win over. I would curse my human weakness and practice more acts of cruelty. I wanted to prove myself worthy of being a disciple for the devil.

...and in those days shall men seek death, and shall not find it and shall desire to die and death shall flee them...

This accounted for my numerous attempts at suicide. I felt that I

125

could not die and would prove my theory with repeated attempts at suicide. My arms were a mass of scars from the numerous cuts on them.

Officer Connie Seabrooks was on duty during one of my suicide attempts. I took a piece of metal that I had found and sliced it deep into my arm. Blood began to spurt from the wound. Officer Seabrooks rushed into my cell to stop the blood until medical could arrive. She was a compassionate woman and took her cue from Dison by making light of a serious situation in order to help me keep a grip on my sanity. She would talk with me occasionally. She told me, teasingly, that I was indebted to her. I assumed that she meant for saving my life.

"Oh, I wouldn't have died," I assured her. "I can't die, I'm infallible."

"I'm not talking about saving your life, I'm talking about my new shoes. I just bought them and you bled all over them. They are ruined." We both laughed. She teased me good-naturedly for years.

My obsession with this belief added to the terror most of the staff already held toward me and I enjoyed their terror. Dison felt that this was another phase and that I would soon be tired of it. No one really realized how close to the edge I truly was.

In 1976 I was able to get some information on the side effects of the drug Thorazine smuggled to me by another inmate. I sent this information in a letter to a federal judge. Judge L. Clure Morton treated my letter as a petition and set me a court hearing.

Captain Dison delivered the court's notice. "Here Lee, you are suppose to open this up in front of me and read it," he announced as he handed me the legal mail.

I opened the letter but was confused as to what it meant. "I don't understand it," I said and handed the letter to Captain Dison.

His face showed consternation as he read the document and nodding he handed the letter back to me. "Well by-damn, it looks as if we are going to court." he laughed.

In the weeks that followed Captain Dison told me that Warden Bernhardt wouldn't allow him to testify at the hearing. "She says I'll just get up there and get mad and cuss out the judge or someone," he explained.

On the day of the hearing, Warden Bernhardt, two correctional officers, a woman from Human Resources and I all traveled in the same car to the Federal Courthouse. Judge Morton was a wiry looking man who combed his hair flat against his skull. He listened intently while the warden testified as to why I was being kept heavily medicated.

"Miss Dortch has a long history of mental illness," she explained. "She can present a danger to others as well as herself. The medication is used at the doctor's orders and under the doctor's supervision."

"I have no intention of second guessing a doctor," the judge said. "But it appears that the medication that has been prescribed is for someone who is psychotic. If Miss Dortch is psychotic, then it would appear that the women's prison is not a suitable place for her and she should be placed in a mental facility."

"I don't think she is classified as psychotic but she certainly has severe mental disorders. We have talked with Central State and they will not take her," Warden Bernhardt explained.

I remembered Captain Dison telling me that information in earlier years.

"Are there no other facilities available for her?" the judge asked.

"Deberry Mental Institution is suppose to have a ward for women but we have never needed the space and the men have utilized the ward for the past few years."

"Well, I suggest that some arrangements be made to ensure that the women in need of mental health while they are incarcerated receive it. Now, as to Miss Dortch's complaint of the massive doses she is being administered...."

"We are in the process of reducing her doses." Warden Bernhardt explained.

I caught the word 'process' and smiled. The doses had been reduced only after I had received notice of the upcoming hearing.

Warden Bernhardt was dismissed from the witness stand and the state called the woman from the Department of Human Resources.

The judge only listened to the beginning of her statement before interrupting her. "Excuse me, but have you ever talked with the plaintiff?" he asked in a piqued voice.

The woman blinked in surprise before replying, "No, sir."

"I don't think we will need your testimony. You may step down," the judge ordered.

I was impressed with the authority that the judge had over these people of power and his ability to cower them.

The state called the institution's psychologist and the correctional officers to testify. Then the hearing ended and the judge made his ruling.

He determined that if the institution considered me in need of the massive doses of medication, then I was in need of housing elsewhere—in a facility that could handle my mental health problems. He also ruled that I was not to be given any medication against my will and that I did not have to talk with the psychologist if I chose not to.

I was ecstatic. I had won. The staff were furious. Many predicted that I would kill everyone who came near me in a year's time.

I was determined that for the next year—until my next review hearing—I was going to get control of my life. I was determined there would be no more outbursts of violence. Not being on the medication helped in controlling my outbursts, but some of the medication had long-term side effects, and I would still have moments of unexplained attacks of fear or violence. I think now that these attacks were triggered by the hormone changes in my body caused during the menstruation cycle. In any event, any violence I inflicted that year I inflicted on myself—in an area of my body that would not be noticed by staff.

At the next review, I was still denied being released from my cell. I was full of disappointment. I felt all my efforts had been in vain. I had been locked down for nine years. I wanted out.

I made several attempts at getting messages to the warden to talk with her. She either did not receive my messages or refused to acknowledge them. The familiar cloud of depression began to smother me. I would never be able to escape the tomb that I was forced to live in. I felt so alone and desperate. I knew I was losing control but I was powerless to stop it.

On my thirty minute exercise period I walked up to Officer Gore, a young black female officer, who was sitting in the lobby. "I need to talk with you, I have a problem," I said.

The woman was a kind woman with genuine concern for the inmates. "We don't want anyone to be unhappy," she said as she stood up and started walking with me.

When we had crossed the room I pulled out a shank made from a razor and held it against her neck. "If you say anything to alert someone you are dead," I whispered and guided her down the hall.

As I passed Sharon, an inmate that I frequently talked with through my wicket, I motioned for her to follow. She looked up surprised but she obeyed my command.

We made our way to Sharon's room and I ordered her to tie up Officer Gore with a belt while I moved the furniture against the door, making a barricade. Sharon pleaded with me not to hurt Officer Gore.

"I don't intend to hurt anyone. I only want to talk with the Warden," I assured her.

Officer Gore trembled in fear when I held the razor against her throat and barked my demands to the officers that lined the halls.

Ron Bishop, who had been my counselor since my arrival and was aware of my violence had just been promoted to Warden of Security. His clumsy attempt at getting control of the situation was to remove the electrical socket cover in the next cell and put a gun through it to shoot me. Fortunately he was unable to get a clear shot of me without risking hitting Officer Gore.

I demanded to see Warden Bernhardt. She showed up in less than an hour—her hair still in rollers and her clothes looked as if she had grabbed the first things she saw and pulled them on, heedless of the wrinkles or if they coordinated in color. "Lee, I'm here," she called to me. "But I'm not going to talk with you until you let my officer go."

I pondered her proposal and agreed. "Okay, hold your fire, I'm sending her out," I called back. While Sharon moved the furniture from the door, I continued to call to the Warden. "I tried to talk to you all day. I can't understand why I am never going to be allowed to come out into population."

"Lee, you are mistaken. We are planning on letting you out but a program needs to be established before we can make that decision," she lied in an effort to pacify me.

The lie angered me. I was there at the hearing and I remembered what was said in my presence.

"You liar," I accused.

Officer Gore winced at the anger in my voice. She was afraid that I might explode in violence. Sharon began to kiss my cheek and pat my face in an effort at calming me.

"You promised you would release my officer if I came to talk to you."

"I'll release her," I hissed. "Unlike you, I do not lie."

I pushed the rest of the furniture from the door. Officer Gore started through the door but then she hesitated and turned back.

"What about Sharon?" Her voice full of concern.

I could hear the officers in the hall whispering for her to come out. "I'm not leaving until Sharon leaves," Officer Gore insisted.

"Go ahead," I motioned to Sharon.

Sharon was quick to realize that when she and Gore left, I would be clear for the officers to open fire on me. She began to pat and kiss on me, coaxing me to give her the razor. I gave her the razor and she threw it out. "She is unarmed," Sharon called and she and Officer Gore left the room. Officer Gregory called to me. "Lee come on out with your hands up. Don't lower them."

I moved to the door and raised my hands. When I entered the hall, I was surrounded by the officers and handcuffed. The officers pushed me to the dry cell. I had terrorized the staff so badly that they were afraid that merely locking me in the dry cell would not be sufficient. They thought that I had to be chained and handcuffed to the bed to keep me from coming through the steel door and block walls.

Sharon was also locked down but Officer Gore insisted that she had no part in taking her hostage and explained how Sharon's action had probably contributed in saving her life. Sharon was released and no disciplinary action was taken against her.

The chains and handcuffs were taken off the next day but I remained in the dry cell for three more months. Any show of violence would result in me being handcuffed back to the bed. I managed on several occasions to break the handcuffs. My show of strength only added to the staff's terror and enforced their beliefs that I was a wild animal and should be treated as such.

After repeated requests from Warden Bernhardt, Deberry Mental Institution finally opened up the section for women. It was decided that the Tennessee Prison for Women had no control over me. Since I was refusing the medication, the staff was afraid of me. They no longer could give me enough medication to put me out. It was ordered that I should go to Deberry with the hopes that they could better deal with me. I was chained and handcuffed and taken to Deberry by bus with several other female inmates who had enough emotional problems that they could be considered classified.

CHAPTER 10

Deberry Correctional Institution
Nashville, Tennessee 1979—1983

Most of the women who were transferred to Deberry were suicidal. The rest were misfits who had a combination of emotional problems, ranging from habitual liars to hypochondriacs. In order to open up a women's ward a minimum amount of patients were required, so many of the women had been allowed to volunteer for transfer to this institution. When we arrived at Deberry, we were all orientated as a group by Warden Love.

"I am sure that you are all aware that the men are housed at this institution. Most of these men have sex related crimes, of which I am equally sure that you are aware. Therefore, you women will be restricted to the women's ward. You will not be allowed on the grounds unless accompanied by an officer. Your dining area and recreational room are located on the wing in which you are housed. We want to give you as much freedom as possible without jeopardizing your safety. Housing the women here is a new program and we will have to play it by ear. We have a rule book which we will pass out to each of you later. We expect you to read it and obey the rules. We welcome any input you may have concerning this program. I am available to each of you if, at any time, you wish to talk with me. The counselors are here for your benefit and we expect you to attend the sessions with the counselors."

Warden Love was a slim woman with naturally red hair. She dressed casually and ran her institution just as casually—but efficiently.

After orientation, she spoke with me in her office. "Lee, your reputation has preceded you. I must admit, many of the staff mem-

132

bers have a lot of apprehensions concerning housing you. I also have to admit that the information I received concerning your appearance has been greatly exaggerated. I am hoping that your behavior has been exaggerated as well and I will not have the problems that my staff and I were expecting."

"What did you expect...some wild animal?" I asked.

"Frankly, yes. I received information that best described a wild man in a circus...but that is not important. You appear neat and well mannered. You are articulate. What is important, is that I won't be locking you down. You will be allowed to live in population with the other female inmates. I am doing this against the advice of others in authority and if you present a threat to the institution or to the other inmates, I will have no choice but to lock you down. My aim is to help. I can't do that if I lock you down. I don't think you will let me down. More so, I hope you won't let yourself down."

With that, I was dismissed and returned to the ward. I had to pass through steel, locked doors before reaching it. A security camera was anchored above the door. When the officer saw you, the doors were popped open by a switch for you to enter. Single size metal cots lined both sides of the ward. Our beds had been assigned in advance but there was no problem with moving our sleeping arrangements around as long as we reported the move to the officer. I was content with my bed assignment. I had been assigned the end bed, nearest the recreational area. A small table sat by each bed. There were no lockers to store our clothes so we were instructed to fold our clothes and place them in boxes and slide them under our beds.

Two counselors' offices and a nurses' station also occupied the floor. We were encouraged to talk with the counselors. Group sessions were scheduled and we were all encouraged to participate. We went to the dining area, housed on the ward, together.

I remained pretty much a loner. I attended the group sessions and watched the television in the recreational area or worked out on the gym equipment. I didn't have any close friends. After a few weeks, I noticed a female officer who appeared to be taking a special interest in me. She was a small black woman with finely sculptured features. Her name was Jewell—the name fit her perfectly. She was as beautiful as a jewel. She spent a lot of time in the recreational area when I was there. I watched her as she played pool with some of the other inmates. She would strike a pose when she thought I was looking. The top button on her shirt was usually unbuttoned and when she leaned over the pool table to make a shot, the roundness of her breast would be exposed. Once, when she caught me staring, she winked and made sure that I had many more chances to catch a glimpse of a little cleavage.

We began talking and she began to bring me in food items or let me get things from the kitchen.

I was flattered by the attention this woman was bestowing on me. It never dawned on me that she was drawn to my reputation. I realize now, that the danger I represented excited her. At the time I was so starved for someone to care about me that I fell head-over-heels in love with her and thought her to be equally in love with me.

All institutions that I have ever been in are full of petty jealousies. This institution was no different. Debra, a black inmate, was one of the ones that was jealous of the relationship that I had with Jewell. Debra claimed to be butch but on the street she had five children. She swore that she had been raped all five times but I suspected that her homosexuality was something she used solely for the purpose of entertainment while incarcerated. Debra would watch me when I worked out on the exercise equipment. She had attempted several times to work up to the speed that I had mastered on the speed-bag. She would make snide remarks under her breath in an effort at riling me. She figured if she aggravated me enough that I would explode in a fit of violence and be locked down and she could begin a courtship of Jewell herself. I suspected what she was doing and ignored her taunts, determined that nothing was going to shatter my happiness.

Warden Love began to suspect our relationship and confronted me. I admitted I was attracted to Jewell but told her it was strictly one-sided. I realized that Warden Love was very naive; I hoped that if I told her how Jewell was helping me adjust to being in population, she would overlook any rumors of our lesbian relationship.

134

I rattled on for several minutes. "Jewell has worked with me a lot, I have always been prone to violence but she keeps me calm. When I have periods of depression she is able to talk with me."

Warden Love was not to be taken in by my manipulations. "We can appreciate Jewell's efforts in helping you, but Jewell is not a counselor, nor does she have any training in that field. I do not think it is good for her to continue with these, so called, counseling sessions. Therefore, I am going to assign her a different unit to work."

Jewell was transferred to work in the mailroom. I was devastated but we agreed that we could write letters back and forth. It was against the rules for inmates to write staff, so I arranged for my sister's oldest son to receive my letters to Jewell and re-mail them for me.

When I began to receive rumors from other inmates that Jewell was having a relationship with the inmate in the mailroom, I was terrified. I did not want the rumors to be true. I questioned Jewell in my letters but she assured me that she was being faithful to me, that I was her true love, and a string of other soupy cliches.

I found out that the inmate, whom Jewell was accused of seeing, also worked in the legal library. The mailroom was off limits to the women inmates but the law library was not. I made a shank from a razor blade and a toothbrush and tucked it in my belt. I arranged to have the officer take me to the library. There, I confronted the inmate.

"I hear that you are having an affair with Jewell," I stated.

The man was a tall black man. He stood a good foot taller than me. He was caught off guard with my question but quickly regained his composure and stared down his nose at me. "I don't feel that that is any of your business," he told me coldly.

I was not intimidated by his size. "Well, I think it is. Because she tells me that she is in love with me and I am hearing rumors that she is seeing you. I heard that the two of you sneak off to the storage room above the mailroom. Is this true?"

I could tell that my words had surprised him. "She was seeing you?" he questioned.

"Yes, that was the reason for her transfer."

"Well, she tells me something different," he said slowly.

I realized that he was just as much the victim as I was and there was no point carrying the conversation any further. There was no need for the shank either.

"That's all I want to know," I assured him and left the library.

I was full of hurt and anger. Debra was the first person to cross my path. I am not sure exactly what she said but I heard the name Jewell, and knew by the tone of her voice that she had made a demeaning remark. I was not as willing to ignore her taunts as I had been in the past. I had nothing to lose now.

I reached in my belt and pulled out the shank. With one quick, surprising blow to her gut, I silenced her remarks. Blood spurted from the wounds and I continued walking. I could hear her screams and the officers shouting for assistance from medical.

A few minutes later two officers came to escort me to an isolated cell. I had hidden the shank so no weapon was found on me. Debra refused to say what had happened to her so I was locked down pending an investigation.

Jewell was irate that I had confronted the male inmate, and in an effort at getting back at me, turned some of my letters over to Warden Love. When one of the counselors questioned me about the letters, I felt even more hurt and betrayed. I felt violated because someone else had read personal letters to someone I loved. I was full of so much anger and anguish. I needed to see or talk with Jewell. I couldn't think of any way to get her to come to my cell.

When Officer Bandy brought me my dinner one evening, I decided to take her hostage. "Now don't be afraid," I told Officer Bandy as I grabbed her from behind, holding her arm with one hand and using my other arm to hold her around the neck. "I'm not going to hurt you, but I want to use your walkie-talkie."

The officer blinked and nodded. I took that to mean she was not going to give me a hard time and grabbed her walkie-talkie and used it to demand to see Jewell.

Captain Donald Campbell answered my demand by ordering me off the radio.

"It seems to me that I am the one who will do the ordering," I returned.

When Captain Campbell realized that I was not going to listen to anyone until Jewell would talk with me, they agreed to my demands by putting Jewell on the radio. "Lee, they won't let me in until you agree to let Officer Bandy go and give your word not to do me any harm."

I promised and Jewell was allowed to exchange places with Officer Bandy.

"Why are you pulling this goddamn stunt?" she demanded in a coarse whisper because she was aware that the other officers were outside the cell listening.

"Because you turned my letters over to Warden Love."

Jewell was quick to cover herself. "I thought you had an officer mail them and I was afraid that it would get out that you were mailing letters to me," she lied. "I only turned some of them over to the Warden just in case she found out and wondered why I had not turned the letters in."

"Ha," I snorted. "The post mark is Arkansas. I had my nephew mail them. You're lying...you turned them over so you would look good."

She pleaded with me, still assuring me that she didn't know I would get so angry. She had only turned in the letters that weren't personal and promised she would never do it again.

I released Jewell and the Captain wrote me a discipline. I was locked down for thirty days and released back into population. I did not continue my relationship with Jewell. I realized that she hadn't loved me as I had loved her. Jewell was later terminated after a staff member caught her and the inmate from the mailroom together.

I did not seek any other relationships. I was very lonely but I also realized I needed to avoid emotional commitments—especially stormy relationships—if I was ever to get a grip on my sanity. My mental stability progressed over the next few years. I wasn't taking the medication and I seemed to be able to control my outburst's more. I don't know how I knew the medication was the cause of most of my violence but I felt I was progressing and I wasn't as afraid of unexplained fears.

I was encouraged to take a special group session with one of the

137

counselors. Actually there was only one other patient in the session and he was a male patient. He was also into self-mutilation and the counselor felt that we might have a common bond and could discuss our fears and frustrations.

When I learned that the man had been convicted of rape and killing a young woman, I refused to continue the sessions. "I don't want to be around that crazy," I told Thelma Camp, the counselor.

"Why, Lee? Do you think you are better, because your emotional condition is different than his?"

"Yes, I'm not a rapist," I retorted piously.

"No, you aren't, but what would you have been had you been a male and homosexual? How would you have handled the confusion. Look what a fine looking man he is. Don't you think he could have had a woman willing, if he wanted one? Rapists get little if any sexual satisfaction from the sex act itself. It's the violence they seek. You can certainly understand violence as a form of expressing the confusion you feel, can't you?"

I agreed with her. I continued the sessions and later joined in the larger group sessions. I noted that most of the men with violent crimes were nice looking. I began to realize the frustrations that other homosexuals experienced. I also remembered Bill, my teenage friend who had killed himself shortly after my arrest. I was beginning to feel compassion for the others—an emotion that I had not been able to feel for a long time.

I participated in many group sessions. The counselor encouraged us to call her by her first name—to create a more informal atmosphere. In one of the sessions, Thelma gave each of the patients a lemon. We were instructed to become familiar with the lemon, to understand each wrinkle and knot on it. After we were sure that we were familiar with the lemon, the counselor took the lemons and placed them in a pile. We were instructed to find our lemon. I did not see any purpose in the session but I was sure that I had found my lemon. When Thelma questioned us, we were all sure that we had found our lemon.

"Yes, you are all sure that you have your lemons because you want to be sure. The mind convinces you of what you want to be convinced of—it is the power of suggestion," she explained.

In another session we played a game where each patient had to pretend they were on a train. As the train traveled it made stops; we clapped our hands in a rhythmic beat and, as we moved around the circle, each player had to say the name of a city where their train would stop. The city names had to be in alphabetical order. If you could not think of a name for the letter that you were required to use, then the person on the right could instruct you to do something silly or foolish.

When I missed my stop, the women on my right—who knew my past obsession with the devil—instructed me to recite a Bible verse. I realized she thought that because I did not believe in God, that I did not know the Bible. She had not known that I had read the Bible so many times that I had parts of it memorized. I stared her straight in the eye and recited several verses.

Later Ms. Camp complimented me on my memorization, and I explained my obsession with being the devil's disciple. I wasn't as obsessed with that feeling but I still believed that I had some evil purpose.

"Do you believe in the Devil?" I asked her one day.

"Let's say I believe in evil," she answered. "I believe in the evil of man...but not a supernatural being...not a commander-in-chief with thousands of disciples to do his bidding. What do you believe, Lee?"

"I don't know what I believe. I guess I'm an atheist."

"Only a fool is an atheist. We have to be created by some force, somewhere. I don't think you are an atheist. I think you are agnostic—many people confuse the words. Agnostics believe in power somewhere, but are not convinced that the Christian God is the power. Atheists do not believe in any power at all—good or evil."

"Do you believe in demon possession?"

"No, I think that there is nothing recorded in history that cannot be explained by hysteria or some other mental aberration—the power of suggestion."

Thelma appeared to understand me and to accept me. She would work with me on a one-to-one basis. She understood my outbursts of violence, and encouraged me to release all anger. She would sit quietly, smoking a Pall-Mall cigarette, while I hit metal book shelves or lockers or any piece of furniture I chose to vent my anger on. When I was exhausted, she would bandage my hands and we would talk quietly. Through our talks I discovered I didn't like me and did not feel that anyone else could like or love me. I wanted so desperately to be liked, accepted and loved. I craved attention and would do anything for attention. My acts of violence were a cry for attention. I also learned that I couldn't communicate with people. I was afraid to tell what I really felt for fear of ridicule—I realized I had a phobia of being laughed at or ridiculed.

Thelma suggested we make an agreement or pact. If I would reach certain goals in my behavior, she would reward me. She stuck to her agreement and I would work for the projected goal—eager for praise or approval. The rewards would be small items such as a special brand of cigarettes or a deli-sandwich, but these items were special to me. She kept a record on my behavior in an effort to negate some of the unfavorable ones in my file.

I was beginning to feel emancipated. There were still angry outbursts or periods of depression but I felt stronger emotionally.

I continued in this way and in 1983 I returned to the main women's prison. Captain Dison had suffered a stroke and had retired. Warden Bernhardt had moved to another position in the Department of Corrections, and Warden Eileen Radeker had taken her position.

Her administration was stricter, less humane. Her staff were promoted by the amount of disciplines that they wrote against inmates. The segregation units that usually held one or two inmates in the past, were now packed with twenty or thirty inmates housed for punishment. Officers wrote disciplines over petty issues. If an officer didn't write a discipline or showed too much compassion for an inmate, they were terminated. Cruel or unprofessional conduct was ignored. If a situation arose where it could not be ignored then the officer was transferred to another institution. Very seldom was the officer terminated. Promotions were rapid. A correctional officer could move up to administrative staff in a few short years, without benefit of additional education. Many correctional officers were able to advance to even higher positions in the Department of Corrections. Nepotism was very common. In some instances a whole family worked the same shift. If you displeased an officer then you displeased the rest of his family. You could have eight or ten officers who were after your neck.

Many privileges were taken away. Inmates in the past had only been required to wear the uniforms during work hours and were allowed to wear their personal clothing at other times. Under Radeker's administration the uniforms were worn at all times outside the cell.

For many inmates, prison would be their home for several years. Pride was taken in decorating their cell rooms with matching bed spreads, throw rugs, and curtains sent from home. The wardens in the past had considered it good for morale. Warden Radeker considered it coddling prisoners and ordered all personal linens to be sent home. Curtains were removed as she considered it a fire hazard. Her coldness was reflected in her officers. All inmates were considered as sub-level humans. A higher fence was installed around the institution, set in a double row with razor wire across the top. Officers were assigned to ride perimeter patrol to keep inmates from even thinking about escape. There had never been a high escape rate in the past.

Before long I found myself locked down again. The isolation was devastating and I suffered a setback in my emotional stability. I knew I couldn't live any longer like a caged animal. I had another inmate, who was also in segregation, agree to leave her medication in the shower. I would retrieve it during my shower time. When I had hoarded a lethal dose, I made my decision to end the torment forever.

The dose did the trick. My heart stopped. There wasn't any bright light at the end of the tunnel like it had been reported. There was nothing. The para-medics were able to get my heart beating again, but I couldn't be transported to a hospital because a guard couldn't be called off a post to accompany me. Officer Rudy Lyles, who was working perimeter patrol, parked the patrol vehicle and volunteered to go as a guard. When he was cautioned by other staff that to abandon his position could mean dismissal, his comment was that he had a higher authority to answer, and that his God considered a life worth saving, no matter to whom it belonged.

Three days later, I woke up in ICU at General Hospital. The realization that I was still alive—that I had botched my death—was devastating. I had no will to go on.

Officer Lyles thought I was his personal responsibility and would tease me every chance he got. I realize now he was using the same tactic—making light of a serious situation—that Dison and Seabrooks had used to help me get a grip on my sanity. He would compliment me on how pretty I was and that I should let my hair grow out. I was embarrassed by his attentions, and would immediately fly into a snit, and order him to mind his own business. He would laugh mischievously.

He continued his playful banter for several months, then we received news that he had died unexpectedly from a heart attack while working under his car. Both staff and inmates were surprised when they read his obituary in the newspaper and learned he was a former country-western singer. He had been a wealthy man, even owning his own airplane. He had worked at the prison to settle an emotional debt.

I had a warm feeling for this man—like he was sent to be my guardian angel. I have never been a religious person but I hoped that this man's part in saving my life wiped his slate clean before he met his maker. This feeling of concern was another emotion that I had not experienced for a long while.

My suicide attempts were still frequent. I can look at the reports in my record now and see that the suicide attempts occurred on a regular basis. This further supports my belief that my menstrual cycle triggered the side effects of the drugs that I had been administered in the past—which resulted in my emotional instability. Of course, I was not aware of PMS nor any other form of chemical imbalance, nor the changes that occur when you reach menopause, but I was aware that there were changes in me.

After my eleventh suicide attempt in thirteen months, Warden Radeker decided she was going to 'break' me from these suicide attempts. She devised a program where I was to be placed in the dry cell for an extended amount of time. I would not be allowed any contact with anyone, including the guards. The staff was forbidden to talk to me—even to answer a question. All my clothes were taken away and I was provided with a blanket and a paper gown. I was denied out-going mail and all my incoming mail was held at the administration building. I wasn't allowed any writing material and only one book a week. My exercise period was at midnight in the lobby. I would lie in the isolated cell unaware of the time of day, whether it was day or night or how many days had gone by. I tried to judge the time and day by the staff members who were working the shift but I still felt that I was in the twilight zone or hell.

Most of the staff were 'job-scared' so they kept to the letter of the program. Others expressed their concerns to me and compared the harshness of the administrator's decision with a Gestapo attitude. I agreed with them. One evening I called from the wicket to an officer several times. When she continued to ignore me, I finally told her she would have been a perfect officer in Hitler's army. She turned and gave me a cold stony glare, but still did not talk to me.

After several months in the dry cell, I was able to get a message to an inmate to ask her to contact a civil rights group for me. The inmate called American Civil Liberties Union of Tennessee (ACLU). They arranged for their attorney, Gordon Bonnyman, to come talk with me. He helped me file a petition in the Federal Courts for my release.

United States District Judge John T. Nixon condemned the prison's practice of keeping me confined as treatment:

"Punishment characterized as treatment is still punishment and will be judged as such under the constitution. Based on the evidence presented...the courts conclude that the defendant's placement of the plaintiff in seclusion without proper clothing, bedding, or human contact raises grave questions of due process and Eighth Amendment violation. Although characterized by good motives and a desire to provide proper medical treatment to the plaintiff, the defendant's concern for the plaintiff has resulted in imposing on her unconstitutional conditions of confinement."

The petition resulted in a court order being issued to release me. There was a lot of media publicity concerning the harshness of the treatment that I was receiving, and Warden Radeker announced she was leaving her position. Since I was aware that the Department of Correction usually transfers a person when they create public notoriety, I was not surprised at her sudden transfer.

Warden Greer returned to the position that she had been temporarily assigned to when I first arrived.

When I was finally released into population, I was ecstatic. I was given a job as dorm maid. I performed my duties diligently, afraid that any negligence would send me back to segregation.

Under Greer's administration the strict rules and guidelines that had been enforced under the administration of Warden Radeker, were relaxed.

A few months after my release from segregation, the prison provided the inmates with a law library. A position as an inmate law clerk was created. My experiences in the Federal Courts had triggered an interest in the technicality of the law. I had witnessed, first hand, the power the Federal Courts held over the Department of Correction during my hearing on whether medication could be forced on me. I had used the law library at Deberry and my interest had not been diluted. The court-ordered release from the dry cell was further proof of the power of the Federal Courts. I wanted to know more about the complexity of the law. I applied for the position and soon after I received a notice from Warden Greer that I had been accepted.

My interest in the law increased. Burying myself in the mountains of State Codes Annotated, was an outlet for my rage. I began a constant fire of petitions to the Knoxville court, concerning constitutional rights that were denied me during my trial in 1972. I had never been read the Miranda warning, or mentally evaluated to see if I was competent to stand trial. I was also denied effective counsel and I should have never been forced to stand in a line-up with men. I applied my energies just as diligently to the legal research as I had in the past to digging through my cell wall or terrorizing the staff.

There were still moments of panic or feelings of rage but the staff began to realize if I was treated fairly I would return fair behavior. I also gained the reputation that if I gave you my word, I meant it. Some staff still regarded me as an animal, but many began to know me as a human being—with feelings and hurts just like any other human being.

Thelma was still concerned for me. To rehabilitate me would be a feather in her cap. She was instrumental in arranging for me to meet the parole board. She also arranged for me to work with her husband in a sign printing and decal application business, also offering me the use of a guest cottage that was in back of her home.

A few weeks before I was to meet the parole board, I was notified by the warden that I was scheduled to be transported back to Knoxville for a post-conviction review of my constitutional rights. Because of the likelihood that I would not be back from Knoxville to meet the parole board, Thelma needed to know what I planned to do. I was unsure what to do—I hadn't really expected to hear anything on the petitions to the court. I decided to withdraw my petition for post-conviction. My request was granted without prejudice, which meant that I would be able to file again at a later date. To have it postponed or to have my parole hearing postponed never occurred to me. I was too overwhelmed with the idea that I might be released. It had been almost thirteen years since the brief period of my release from Federal custody. In all I had been locked up for over twenty-three years.

Charles Traughber had been the chairman of the parole board during Governor Ray Blanton's administration. The 'Clemency for Cash' investigation had caused plenty of media publicity, and the parole board had been under scrutiny for its approval of clemency. Traughber had been removed from the chairman's position, however he was allowed to remain on the parole panel and he carried a lot of clout with the decision on who made parole—in fact, you couldn't tell he wasn't the chairman.

I remembered Captain Dison mentioning him several years ago when an inmate's husband had been caught attempting to bring drugs into the institution and was denied visiting with his wife. A month later, we heard the inmate being called for visiting.

"I thought he couldn't visit her anymore," I commented.

"Hell, Lee...you know how things like that go. Someone from downtown got him back on her visiting list."

When the inmate later went to a clemency hearing, she came back irately. It seemed her husband had been smuggling cocaine into the institution for her to sell until she had paid enough to the parole board to pay for her clemency. She had gone to the parole board hearing expecting to have her clemency granted—Traughber had promised her clemency.

Marie Ragghainti, another member of the parole board had failed to approve her clemency. Ms. Ragghainti was in the process of initiating a full investigation of the board's practice of recommending clemency to be granted by the governor for a price. The investigation had resulted in many demotions and prosecutions.

The same inmate's clemency hearing was scheduled again without Ms. Ragghianti's knowledge—Charles Traughber was on the panel and the inmate's clemency was granted.

My request for parole was received with mixed emotions by the parole board. Charles Traughber despised me and considered me an animal that did not deserve to be let loose in society. He stated, very vehemently, that I was a vicious and cold-hearted killer. I wondered how Traughber could justify the things he had said to me when he had such an active part in releasing multi-murderers, sex offenders and child molesters who had only served three or four years—sometimes less.

Fortunately, he voted only if the board's decision was split. After four hours of discussion and deliberation, the board voted to grant me parole.

I was released to Thelma. Her children were kind but her husband was a foul-tempered man who could hardly see and suspected every one of being negligent in their duties. His children ran the business and were used to his evil temper, and went about their duties unperturbed.

I, on the other hand, was in constant terror of offending him...not afraid of him physically, for he was a tiny shriveled man, but afraid of the ridicule and verbal abuse he could subject a person to when the mood struck him.

After three months of working with him and walking on eggshells, I finally became the object of his anger. He accused me of leaving bubbles in a decal that I had just applied. I assured him that there were no bubbles and that I had taken my time and performed the task professionally. He refused to admit his poor eyesight would not allow him to see my work and subjected me to a string of insults.

I have never been able to endure embarrassment, I still don't deal with it very well now, and I really couldn't handle it then. I returned his insults with obscenities and ended it with my quitting the job. I stormed back to the guest cottage and packed my few personal belongings. Thelma had encouraged me to save most of my salary and I withdrew it from my savings account. I had no destination in mind.

I only wanted to flee the verbal abuse I had just been subjected to. Thelma had been good to me, but she had made a grave mistake in her judgment about helping me prepare for the transition into society. My work, housing, counseling and social life were all wrapped around her. When my relationship to her household ended, then I was left without any ties to the free world—I was virtually helpless. I had no job, no place to live and no one I could talk with.

I bought a bus ticket to Memphis that night and spent several days with Martha, spending my savings lavishly. Martha finally reminded me of the parole condition of not associating with other felons and expressed her concern for her own parole. Out of sympathy for her I bought a ticket back to Nashville, but I was terrified. I had no one in Nashville that I could go to. The ride on the bus was peaceful—I felt the same security I felt when I was in prison. I felt protected. The closeness of the sides of the bus was soothing— much like controlled environment of the institution and the protected capsule of my cell. I relaxed on the ride.

When I arrived in Nashville, I was full of anxiety. The rush of people hurrying everywhere frightened me. My pulse began to race as I moved to the ticket window to purchase another ticket—to anywhere. I had to be back on the bus, back where someone else was in control and making the decisions of my destination.

The next bus was to somewhere in Mississippi. The cost of the ticket depleted the remainder of my savings. I arrived in the early morning in a rural Mississippi town. The station was on the outskirts of town.

Twenty-three years ago I may have been secure in picking up my baggage and seeking the adventures of the unknown, but after the lengthy years of incarceration, I was frightened of the changes that had taken place in the free world.

Telephones were all touch-tone dialing. The operator assisted calls were a thing of the past, as were the ten-cent telephone calls. I had no idea what a liter of coke was, nor did I understand how the cashier at the grocery store could record the price, simply by moving the items across a glass plate housed in the counter.

When I arrived in the rural town, I was full of anxiety of the unknown. I was afraid I couldn't survive alone.

I began walking. Few buildings were in sight and as I walked, the buildings became more and more scarce. I was beginning to realize I was walking in the wrong direction, when a young black man approached, greeting me in a friendly fashion.

"Hey buddy, you gotta light?" he called. I set my baggage down and produced a book of matches.

I could feel him scrutinizing my face from the light of the match.

"Excuse me," he apologized. "I thought you were a fella."

I accepted his apology, still aware of his scrutiny, and the fear began rising to my throat.

"You kinda walking in the wrong direction ain't you?" he asked benevolently.

"Ahhh…" I drawled, at a lost for words.

"Town's thata way," he motioned with his thumb.

"Thanks," I answered in embarrassment. "I was beginning to realize I was going the wrong direction."

"Where you headed, anyway?" the stranger persisted.

"Nowhere, I just arrived and thought I would look the place over. I might settle in, if I like it here."

The stranger looked at me questioning again. "Well, come on with me. I can introduce you to some of the town's folks," he offered.

I was leery of going with the stranger but more leery of going on alone. I accepted his invitation. We walked to a honky-tonk in a black neighborhood. As this black man entered with a white stranger, a hush fell over the room.

"Relax," he laughed. "She's not the law."

The noise level rose again as if on cue. We made our way to the far side of the bar where he introduced me to the female owner. She

148

agreed to let me stay on and do odd jobs for room and board.

After a few days of living in the honky-tonk, I came to the conclusion that I didn't like being free. The loud music and laughter grated on my nerves. No one ever slept or let you sleep. It was wild and noisy for twenty-four hours a day. I craved the protection of the prison, where you were told when to sleep and when to wake up. You didn't have to worry about not being accepted in society. I wanted to go back to what I had been used to for twenty-three years—I wanted to go back to prison. I didn't have anyone to call for help.

Part of my parole condition had been to go to counseling, but I had convinced Thelma that it was unnecessary. In turn, she had assured my parole officer that she was qualified to handle any crises I might have. The parole officer had agreed and had not insisted on counseling.

I had discontinued any correspondence with my family years ago—when I thought I had been chosen to do the devil's bidding. After Mama died, I had not tried to re-established any communication with them and had the misguided feeling that they did not want me to communicate with them. I had always been an embarrassment to them and thought that they were probably glad to be rid of me.

I called the Warden of Treatment at the Tennessee Prison for Women and begged her to help me. I wanted to return. I didn't have anywhere else to go.

She recognized the terror in my voice and told me she would see what she could do. I was to call her again in two hours. I began to drink while I waited the two hours. When I called her back, I was thoroughly drunk.

"Lee, have you been drinking?" she asked me.

"Yes," I confessed in a slurred voice.

"Lee," she cautioned, "you are only adding to your troubles...now listen to me closely. We can't take you back...this is not a hotel and you have not violated your parole as far as we are concerned. I am trying to arrange for a half-way house to take you, but I can't do anything in the middle of the night. You need to come back to Tennessee and we will see what we can do."

149

I began to cry. "I'm broke, I can't return to Tennessee."

"Calm down...Right now, that is the least of your problems. I will arrange for you to have a ticket at the bus station." she promised and hung up the phone.

When I arrived in Nashville, I contacted her again. She hadn't been able to find a place for me, but she assured me she was still working on it.

I panicked and decided to take matters in my own hands. I left the phone booth in search of a victim. I spotted a nurse leaving a hospital and walking towards her car. I approached her and before she was able to scream, I threw my arm around her and held a knife against her throat. I hadn't intended on cutting her, but she began to struggle and I pushed her away from me. The sharp blade of the knife nicked her skin. She turned and gave me a terrified stare before quickly running to another car that was pulling out of the parking lot. I watched her as she jerked the car door open and jumped in. I could see her hysterically explaining to the startled citizen what had happened. I began to walk in the opposite direction. As I walked, a patrol car pulled along side of me. The wheels rubbed the sidewalk. "Lee Dortch," the officer called, "you need to get in the back seat."

I obeyed silently.

"Want a cigarette?" he offered. "The prison called to alert us that you were drunk and upset," he said as I reached for the cigarette. "I was on my way over here to check on you when I heard the call about the assault...was that your doing?"

"What about Miranda warning?" I asked coldly.

"You're not under arrest," he assured me sincerely. "We are just talking. Lee, I'm sorry I was too late."

I remained silent. I was scared and felt vulnerable. The compassion this man was showing me was making me wimp-out. I felt sorry for myself and I wanted to cry—but not where this man could see me.

Another patrol car, answering to the assault call, pulled beside us. "I've got this under control," the officer assured him and we pulled off in the direction of the jail.

I was driven to the police station and booked and finger-printed. None of the matrons wanted to strip search me due to my masculine appearance, so I was locked into an isolated cell with no running water. As I sobered up and my thirst increased, I was enraged at my mistreatment and began to raise hell. My protests were all ignored.

When the officer from the Parole Board arrived to arrange for a revocation hearing on my parole, I demanded in front of the deputies to know why I was being held in a cell that had no water. The parole officer looked at the deputy who had brought me from my cell to the conference room, asking for clarification.

"We weren't aware that there wasn't any water in the cell, but we will see to it that she is moved immediately," he assured the parole officer.

After my conference with the parole officer and the date for a revocation hearing was set, I was taken to the courtroom for arraignment.

"I want a psychological evaluation," I demanded of the judge.

The judge ignored my demands. He knew as well as I did, that to get a psychological evaluation before I was sentenced would mean I would be housed for thirty days at Central State. He also knew that Central State did not utilize fences or locked cells. I am sure he suspected that after I had sobered up, I grew to regret my foolish action and now, did not look forward to returning to prison, and that I was manipulating for an escape.

He looked at me sternly, noting my masculine appearance and studied the nurse, who was my accuser, over the top of his glasses. He also noted the tiny, squirrel-looking husband in leg braces and asked vehemently, "Is this a lover's quarrel?"

The nurse's husband blinked three times quickly, which caused him to look even more like a squirrel, before defending his wife's honor. He protested that they had never seen me before in their life.

"Bull shit," the judge growled.

I took pity on the couple's dilemma and confirmed their claims. "They are right your honor, I had never seen any one of these two before that night."

The judge was full of skepticism, but he didn't pursue the subject any further and bound me over for grand jury.

151

I was moved to a bay unit with other female inmates. The fact that I had never been strip searched was ignored. I remained in the jail for three days. I still refused to plea bargain until after I was psychologically evaluated. The judge finally ordered for me to be transported back to the prison to await trial. There, I was locked in segregation for thirty days and then released into population. I still held out on plea bargaining for another year and finally agreed to six years for assault.

CHAPTER 11

Tennessee Prison for Women

When I arrived back at the Tennessee Prison for Women, I was full of shame that I had not been able to make it in the free world. Many people asked me questions about my short time out but I refused to answer. Through rumors and gossip, a reputation for my wanting to live out my life in prison grew. I had already served more time than any other woman in the history of Tennessee. As time passed and my story was told again and again, it became more ominous. The newspaper coverage painted a colorful description of me which added to my reputation.

When I had been on parole, one of Thelma's sons had taken me with him to do some target practice. The whole family had boasted a fine gun collection, including machine guns. He had taken a picture of me with these guns strapped across my chest like a terrorist. The pictures had been taken from me after I returned to prison, but this simple picture was used to fuel the rumor that I had been a party to illegal gun trafficking. I was not aware of many of these rumors but my shame and embarrassment caused me to alienate myself from most people. My quiet reserve added to the awe that surrounded me.

People at other institutions and county facilities heard of my reputation and many convicted felons were warned about me prior to being transported to the prison. New inmates approached me for advice about criminal activities inside the institution. I chose to remain alone which added to the aura around me.

On one occasion—for a brief period—I did consent to assist in selling of drugs inside the institution. An inmate who had been released on parole would send me packages with the contraband hidden discreetly in the hems and seams of clothing or in the heels of shoes. I would sell the drugs and mail out her cut of the money. I asked for the position as laundry aide so that I would have freedom of movement to deliver the laundry to inmates as well as the drugs that I sold. I prospered financially and gained a lot of 'friends.' Pam Wilson was one of the friends I gained. She had heard of me in county jail. She was a drug addict and she knew she couldn't survive prison without access to drugs.

Soon after she arrived in prison, I met her in the hall. She pretended to bump into me. When I tried to pass her she was in my way. When I stepped aside, she stepped in my path. I thought the confusion was accidental and we both laughed.

"I'm sorry," she purred. "I'm so clumsy. I just got here and I am so nervous," she explained.

"There isn't any reason to be nervous. It isn't as bad as the prison scenes you see on television," I assured her.

"Oh, I am glad to hear that," she said her voice still sounding like a cat's purr. "I have been so afraid. Say you wouldn't want to kinda show me around would you?"

My ego soared. She was a beautiful girl with honey brown hair that swept her waist. I was more than willing to show her around the prison. We made a date to go to the gym that evening to play cards. Pam spent the evening complimenting me. We made a date to meet for breakfast the next morning. We met every day in the dining room for meals and in the gym in the evenings. We would slip off to the bathroom in the gym for wild, passionate kisses. I ached to have this woman in my arms. I desired her more than any woman I had ever desired in my life.

"I can't go on like this," Pam said breathlessly one evening while we were passionately kissing. "We have to be roommates. You are driving me crazy. I have to be with you...soon," she declared.

I was just as eager to be with her. I couldn't sleep at night for wanting her. The next day I talked to the sergeant about moving. The number of women housed in the institution had increased from sixty-five when I first arrived to three-hundred. Most inmates were being housed two to a cell, unless they could not adjust to living with another inmate. I had never had a roommate—I had never wanted one and most people would have been afraid to room with me. But if I wanted one there was no reason why I couldn't have one. Pam moved into my room three weeks after she arrived in the institution.

I learned that Pam had come from a respectable family, but her drug addiction had forced her to abandon any morals that may have been instilled in her as a child. She had turned to prostitution to support her habit. She knew how to please a man for the greatest profit. She had no problem with pleasing me for the same reason.

I convinced myself that she loved me and wouldn't let myself see her whorish ways in our lovemaking. She wore sheer nighties or would parade around the room nude. She was always ready for lovemaking and received the greatest satisfaction when pain was inflicted. When I first saw her breast, I was horrified. They were scarred with bite marks from past lovers. One nipple was bitten nearly off—it hung by a small piece of skin. She loved to claw my back during our lovemaking and my back stayed a mass of bloody scratches. The pain in our lovemaking sickened me but because it pleased her I faked pleasure.

Our relationship was full of jealousy and accusation. I was acutely aware that Pam would not hesitate to apply the same feminine wiles that sent me bowing at her feet, to a counselor or guard who could provide her with the same gratuities—dope. I forbade her to go to any area of the compound unless I escorted her. I would walk her to work and arrive when she was to get off work to walk her back to our room. I frequently arranged to drop in on her in her work area to dispel any jealous fear that she was with someone else. If her day off was different from mine, I would insist that she stay where I could watch her from the laundry room where I worked. On several occasions I could smell male cologne on her and would confront her. I think she deliberately taunted me with her affairs in the hopes that I would hit her. She delighted in the physical abuse. One evening she told me she had to work late with one of the counselors. As the counselor had his own aide, I thought this was strange. After she left for work, I went to talk with Dianne, the counselor's aide. She did not know anyone was working late.

As I waited for Pam to return, my anger grew. When she returned, I was wild with jealousy.

"Where the hell have you been?" I demanded.

"I told you…I had to work," she answered.

"Don't lie to me, you tramp, Dianne said no one was working over."

"Well Dianne must have lied," she said and moved to put her arms around me.

I pushed her aside. I didn't want her to be near me. She returned and tried once again to put her arms around me. This time I pushed her back on the bed with great force. I could see my rage was exciting her and it disgusted me. She began to unbutton her shirt and ran her hands across her breast in a seductive manner.

"You know I haven't been with anyone. A man can't please me like you can," she said, her voice thick with passion.

I was further disgusted with her attempt at seducing me but at the same time aroused by her.

"I can smell that damn man on you," I hissed and grabbed her by the arm, jerking her to her feet. "You had better be glad that I don't kill you both. Go shower…I don't want the smell of that man in this room," I said through gritted teeth and shoved her toward the door.

She obeyed, and when she returned our love making was wild and frantic—full of hate and violence.

This was one of many quarrels. My confrontations would lead to each hurling insults at the other. Our fights became more frequent, ending with Pam apologizing, in exchange for a hit of dope.

Five months after Pam moved into my room, a memo was posted that Warden Greer would be leaving and that Warden Radeker would be returning to her position. Rumor was that this action was a result of a lawsuit filed by Warden Radeker concerning her prior transfer. The strict rules were soon re-established and enforced.

Radeker deemed our relationship emotionally unhealthy and arranged for Pam to be sent to an annex of the institution where minimum security inmates were housed.

Before Pam was to receive notification of the transfer, I was locked down while her belongings were packed by staff. I paced the floor of my locked cell while Pam and her belongings were being loaded in a van to be transported. I watched through the small window in the cell door that was used for the staff to count inmates or to monitor their activities. Finally, when the rage at what I considered unfair treatment erupted, I slammed my fist through the glass.

The blood spurted from the cuts in my hand and arm but I ignored it as I tried to reach the knob to the outside of the door. My efforts were useless.

I was taken to medical where my arms were bandaged and then I was locked back into my cell.

Pam's stay at the annex was short. We wrote letters back and forth until she was able to 'cop a discipline,' which, by policy, would require her to be moved back to the main compound. I wanted to believe that she wanted to be near me just as much as I wanted to be with her, but drugs were her motivation. Things didn't go as we had planned. She was locked in segregation and I was unable to get near her, which was my main concern. Her main concern was that I couldn't get drugs to her as fast as she wanted them. Occasionally, I managed to get some of the officers to take her something but the deliveries were not frequent enough for her.

I tried several attempts to get a discipline for myself in the hopes of being locked down in segregation. I spent many hours in a restricted area, calling to the segregation unit. Officers would chase me away but would not write me any disciplines. I look at it now and see how foolish my actions were. I had spent years trying to get out of segregation and now I was trying to get them to put me back in.

On one occasion, I walked up to a security guard and said, "I think Lee Dortch should be searched for contraband."

The officer looked at me in exasperation and began patting me down. She found the 'rig' that I had wanted her to find.

"I guess you will have to write me a discipline, won't you?" I smirked.

The officer wrote me the discipline. Possession of a hypodermic syringe is an 'A' infraction, however, the discipline board determined it to be a minor offense. Instead of locking me in the segregation unit, I was locked in my cell room for five days.

After several weeks of this kind of foolishness, I was shocked when I was suddenly placed in a dry cell for a minor offense. Internal affairs began an investigation of threats that I had allegedly made on the life of a counselor.

I was handcuffed and shackled and heavily guarded each time that I had to be taken to the administration building for interrogations.

Pam was moved to a minimum security institution in Chattanooga, which was her home town where she would have easier access to the drugs she craved. I heard rumors that she was moved because I had made threats on her life as well as on the lives of counselors.

I was confused. Why would anyone think that I had made a threat to her life, I wondered. Then the realization hit me full force. Pam would do anything for drugs. As I wasn't able to keep her supplied with the drugs she craved, she had to resort to more drastic means. The jealous quarrels we had had when she worked for the counselor had been exaggerated and used to her advantage. She wanted to be reclassed to Chattanooga and her ticket there was to say that I had threatened to kill her and the counselor. She would have to be moved to ensure her safety.

After Pam was transported to Chattanooga, I was moved to segregation. I accepted her betrayal but it did little to help on releasing me from segregation. I knew from past experiences with this warden that when she felt she had administered her revenge on me for those petitions I had filed in the federal courts—those which she considered had cost her her job previously—then and only then, would I be released. I was released nine months later.

When I got out of segregation, I was given the laundry-aide position again. I put in for a position as law clerk, but until a position opened I would have to do laundry for new admissions.

I hated the laundry-aide job and put very little effort into seeing it was done properly. Many times, I would pack the washing machine as tightly as possible, with little regard to color and seldom bothering to wait until the officer could issue me soap pow-

158

ders. Then I would run the clothes through half a wash cycle and turn the knob to spin them dry. I would let the wet clothes spin for a brief period in the dryer and then stuff them back into the laundry bags and take them to the inmates. I could usually finish my day's work by nine o'clock in the morning.

After my relationship with Pam, I had decided against any other relationships. I had abandoned my drug selling business and again applied my energies to legal research and resumed my Post Conviction Petition.

Several weeks after I was released from segregation, a new admission came in that I began to notice. Whenever I took her clothes to her, still wet and wrinkled, she would thank me for my efforts. Her face showed that she thought I was incapable of doing better.

I noticed that a few weeks after her arrival, she was paying commissary to the laundry-aide on another hall to do her laundry. This suited me fine. It was one less load of laundry that I had to fool with.

I later learned her name was Lucy and that she was here for murder. There was a lot of inmate curiosity about her but she stayed aloof from everyone.

I happened to be behind her in the commissary line one afternoon and I began a conversation with her by asking her how much time she had.

"Life," she answered and looked away as if she was expecting someone—not adding any more information to the conversation.

New admissions are usually eager to talk about their crime. Each thinks theirs is the most unique case in history. I regarded her as a bit haughty. I proceeded to ask questions attempting to knock her off her high horse. I pointed out that to have a life sentence, she had to have murdered someone. "Who did you kill?" I prodded.

I could tell she didn't want to answer my questions and I was enjoying her discomfort.

"They say my brother-in-law," she answered in a piqued tone.

"How did you do it...shoot him?" I asked with amusement, thoroughly enjoying toying with her.

She gave me a look that was meant to dismiss me from the face of

159

this planet. "They say I strangled him," she stated with a resolute air.

I looked at her tiny, lady-like hands, knowing that her statement was meant to intimidate me.

"Humph...must have mighty strong hands," I laughed, turning to the conversation behind me in an effort to show her I was not impressed.

Several weeks later, I was taken back to Knoxville for a hearing on the petitions I had filed to reinstate my Post Conviction. The hearing was postponed for three months. When I returned to the prison, I was assigned the law clerks position. I was amused to learn that Lucy had been given a law clerk position as well, which meant we would work together. I remembered her prissy ways, and was sure she would not to be thrilled to work with me, nor by my haphazard ways.

Evelyn was the librarian aide. She was responsible for checking the books in and out. She was a pious, socialite who spent her time reminding everyone that she was from 'Signet Mountain,' a pretentious neighborhood in Chattanooga. She regarded her sole duty as librarian was to sit behind the librarian's table to check out books. She held little regard for re-shelving the books in any order. She had very few clerical skills, as her source of income in the free world had been to sell cocaine. She had somehow managed to snag a rich man who had moved her to Signet Mountain. After a few years he grew sick of her drug dealings, and had threatened divorce. She had no intention of giving up the life-style her husband had provided her. Instead, she had hired a hit man to kill him. Claiming her husband's death was caused by an irate drug addict, she was not convicted for several years until the Tennessee Bureau of Investigation had an undercover agent make friends with her. She bragged to her new friend of her cleverness in outwitting the law. Now she considered her conviction unfair. She thought her crime of hiring an assassin to murder her husband was trivial, but she was quick to pass judgment on others. She would humiliate inmates she thought were easily intimidated in an effort at making herself feel important.

Evelyn was irate when she learned that I had been assigned to the library. Our supervisor, Eldon Stinson, was a wimpy man that

Evelyn was able to boss around. She insisted that he test me to ensure that I could handle the position. Stinson had the law clerk at one of the men's prisons prepare a legal test for me to take in the hopes that I wouldn't be able to pass it. To cover himself, he had Lucy take the same test but he provided her with the answers. Lucy watched Evelyn and Stinson in quiet disapproval.

I passed the test to the amazement of both Stinson and Evelyn. Evelyn continued to complain to anyone who would listen about how terrible it was that the 'crazy queer' had been classified to the library. She also voiced her opinion that I only wanted to work in the library to meet lovers—as if I had a string of them waiting. I pretended to ignore her remarks and sat silently doing my work in the law office with Lucy. I noticed Lucy watching me on several occasions when Evelyn and Stinson were discussing me. After a few days she began to slam the door to the office when Evelyn began her whining. I was touched that this woman thought she had to protect me from the cruelty of the world.

I found Lucy warm and loving—despite her stand-offish ways. A few weeks after Lucy and I were classified to the library, another inmate named Dorothy was classified to do the cataloging—a job Evelyn should have been doing for the past few years. Dorothy had been struck by lightning and was paralyzed on the left side. The woman was a hard worker despite her handicap and accomplished the task of cataloging in a few weeks. She was a timid woman and self-conscious of her handicap. Evelyn was quick to turn her verbal abuse in the direction of this woman.

"If they are classifying the handicaps to the library, I want to know what my handicap is," she would say to anyone who would listen, and look in my direction and then at Dorothy.

Lucy helped set up a place for Dorothy to work—as far out of Evelyn's range of verbal abuse as she could get.

When Evelyn had repeated the statement several times, Lucy walked to her table, smiled sweetly and said, "Perhaps your attitude Evelyn," and turned on her heels to leave Evelyn with her mouth open like a dying fish. I thought the whole situation was funny.

Lucy was very sweet-natured and easy to get along with. We

were able to learn from each other. My experience with the federal courts gave me an extra advantage in understanding reliefs sought in the federal courts. Lucy recognized this knowledge and did not hesitate to utilize it. I wasn't as familiar with the lower courts and she was eager to share her knowledge with me. We made a good team and were able to provide inmates with the help they needed to address their legal issues.

Lucy stayed to herself but she was well liked by most of the staff members. To the amazement of everyone Radeker—who didn't like anyone—liked her. She liked Radeker as well and did not find her to be harsh or cold. Lucy had the ability to make everyone feel special, but at the same time she kept her distance. She didn't want to become close to anyone. I always felt special in her presence and our friendship grew. Radeker approved of our friendship.

I suspected that Stinson was attracted to Lucy. I watched him jealously while he followed her around like a puppy dog. Lucy was unaware of his attentions but Evelyn noticed. Evelyn resented our friendship and was insulted that Lucy had chosen the 'crazy queer' to be friends with over someone with her obvious social status. Her only explanation for this slight was that Lucy and I must be having a relationship. She began to voice this conclusion to Stinson and the two of them would whisper together like two old women gossiping in the church yard after Sunday services.

This piece of information was received by Stinson as the only logical reason that his attentions to Lucy were being ignored. He began to pick at me—finding fault with all my work. He would make me type memos over several times or give me a direct order to rearrange books and then direct me to put them back in their original place. I tried my best to please him but I realized that was not possible as long as he was being manipulated by Evelyn.

I also found myself falling in love with Lucy. I began to apply my energies to court her. She would laugh merrily when I would ask to hold her hand or shake her head in amusement when I asked for a kiss. I used all my resources to catch her attention—sympathy, intrigue, sexual magnetism.

"You need to quit," she would laugh when I persisted in the

courtship. I wanted to know more about her. I knew it was her nature to protect the underdog and I suspected that trait hadn't begun in prison.

I pulled the *South Western Reporter* from the shelf and read more about her case. I learned that she was convicted of murdering her brother-in-law. Her own husband had been killed in an automobile accident three days before her trial. To me, the case didn't make any sense. There hadn't appeared to be any motive and I wondered about the victim's wife? What part had she played? Lucy's sister, the victim's wife, had inherited over thirty thousand dollars in insurance and had had a lover. She seemed the most logical suspect to me. I began to feel protective toward Lucy. I suspected she was doing time for someone—her sister. I wanted to kill her sister.

I spent as much time with Lucy as I could. I felt so empty when I was away from her. All I could think about was how sweet and precious she was.

Occasionally, I would work the late shift and on some of these occasions Lucy would work late with me. One evening after dinner and head-count, she was excessively slow about getting ready to go back to the library. I waited impatiently while she changed her clothes and then while she called her attorney. My impatience was beginning to show when I asked her for the third time if she was ready. She informed me she had to call her attorney back in ten minutes. After thirty minutes of delay she was finally ready to go to work. I hurried to the library in a stormy mood. I hated to be late for work. Lucy strolled along with me, causing more delay while she read several bulletin boards. After the fourth bulletin board, I grabbed her hand and pulled her the rest of the way to the library.

When I arrived—with Lucy in tow—the library was dark. "What's wrong with the lights?" I asked as I reached out my hand to flip on the switch.

"They're not working," Stinson announced as the room flooded with bright lights.

"Sure they are," I corrected.

Stinson's hand shot out to the light switch. "No they aren't" he said quickly, and flipped them off again—as if I hadn't seen them on.

163

I looked at him as if he had lost his mind and flipped them back on again.

Lucy burst out laughing and a loud "Surprise" rang out from the back of the library.

Tears began to fill my eyes when I realized that Lucy had arranged a surprise birthday party for me—my first and only birthday party. God, how I loved this woman. If I could only make her understand how much.

A few days after the birthday party, I was notified that I was going back to court to hear my Post Conviction Petition. Lucy sensed the verbal battery that I would have to endure and spent many hours preparing me for the ordeal. Her trial was fresh in her mind and she was aware of the cruel words the District Attorney could hurl at a defendant. She wanted me to understand that no matter what the state said or if they made me feel like a vicious murderer or freak, that I was special and unique. Not worthless, but priceless.

I was transported back to Knoxville, fortified with the feeling of being special. The transporting officer was the same officer as on my previous trip to Knoxville. She judged me on the good conduct I had presented to her then and not on my reputation. She chose not to transport me handcuffed and chained—which was the custom of the past. The prison officials were outraged, but the officer pointed out that I was in her custody. That small action, following Lucy's pep talk, went a long way toward building my self-esteem.

When I arrived at the county facility, I was placed in a holding cell until assigned to a unit. Men were seated on one side of the holding cell, women on the other.

After the processing officer had told me to move to the male side several times, he sighed in aggravation. "Mister where are you from?"

"The women's prison," I smiled, acutely aware of his discomfort at the blunder.

"Sorry." he blushed.

After I was processed in, Leah Prewit, the attorney who had been appointed to represent me, briefed me on what to expect when we entered the courtroom. She cautioned me that no matter what the District Attorney said to or about me, I was to remain calm. If I didn't understand a question, I was to ask that it be repeated.

An hour later we were ready to enter the courtroom. Ms. Prewit stated my issues of having not been represented by effective counsel in my 1971 conviction. She noted that my attorney at the time had not arranged for a psychological examination, offering my past mental history as support for the claim that a psychological examination had been needed.

The District Attorney attempted to discredit her claim. He pointed out that my attorney at the time was now highly respectable, had a flourishing practice, and that it was a disgrace to attempt to blacken his reputation with this claim. He also stated that there was no record of my having a mental history except for a hysterical personality (which was another word for homosexuality), that I had committed several crimes in several other states, that I just wanted to get out from behind prison walls for a little sun, and that I would kill again.

Ms. Prewit was quick to refute his statement that I had committed several crimes in other states. She pointed out that I was housed in several states as a federal prisoner for the same crime, and that I had been in a federal hospital for the insane for three years—not a tiny mental hospital for a short period.

After several hours of verbal bat and ball, the judge finally ruled that he would leave the decision up to the appellate court. At that time the transcripts for my 1971 conviction and psychological records could be entered in support of my claim.

With that, my hearing was over and the bailiff escorted me to the elevator to return to the jail area. When the elevator stopped, I walked to a bench to wait until an officer was available to show me to my cell.

I was still upset about the day's proceedings. The viciousness of the District Attorney's words still rang in my ears. I recounted his remarks, "that I wanted out to kill again" bitterly—as if I couldn't kill inside prison. His remark that I only wanted out to get some sunshine was ridiculous. The women's prison looked like a college campus. On summer days, many women could be seen sunbathing.

165

The District Attorney's picture of prison was certainly distorted.

I was only vaguely aware of the activities that were going on about me. A dinner tray was brought to me and I ate some of it, but I had little appetite.

"Lee, what are you doing down here," I heard a voice call in surprise.

"Waiting," I answered innocently.

"Well, you are waiting with the men who are going on the chain-run to the men's prison," she laughed. She called the women's unit and I was sent upstairs.

She was still teasing the male officers who had been preparing to send me to the men's prison when the elevator closed.

I was anxious to return to the women's prison. The strangeness of the last two weeks had exhausted me and I wanted to be back with Lucy. She had written me everyday since I had arrived. She had even mailed me a card before I had left and it arrived at the jail the same day that I had arrived. I thought it was so cute.

Each day I would ask the officer if they were transporting me that day. After several days of hearing, "You aren't logged to be transported today," I tied a sheet to one of my shoes and using it as a lasso, I threw it out the bars of the unit to the officer's desk. After I had dragged the log book to the cell, I penciled in "Transport Lee to the Women's Prison" under the day's date, and threw the log book back on the desk.

When the officer returned, she laughed at my antics. "Relax, Lee, we are going to send you home tomorrow."

Lucy was waiting on a bench outside the administration building when I returned to the prison. I was like a little kid who had been away at camp for the summer and was returning home. I felt secure in seeing her waiting for me.

I returned to my job the next day, eager to be back working with Lucy. We continued to grow closer but the poison air in the library did not change. The tension caused by Evelyn and Stinson was always present. Stinson continued to find fault in my work. Lucy's crusading instinct forced her to come to my rescue by re-doing some of my typing. On occasions, when Stinson wasn't in the library and Lucy and I were working in the law books, she would step behind the shelves, pulling me with her. She would wink at me mischievously and begin to kiss the back of her hand making loud smacking sounds for Evelyn to hear. I joined in her charade and would add an occasional moan. Other times—when she thought she could risk it without a write up—she would let Evelyn see her sit in my lap and play with the back of my neck.

We would laugh later when she recounted to me how Evelyn had begged her to tell her what it was like to be with a woman. When Lucy told her with exaggerated innocence that she didn't know, Evelyn stomped off in a snit. Our playfulness added to our friendship—a friendship that infuriated both Evelyn and Stinson.

The two of them joined forced against the two of us. When their bullying moved from silly gossip to viciousness, we decided that the only way to stop them was to file a formal grievance. It stated Stinson and Evelyn's prejudice and their unfair treatment toward anyone that they considered below their standards.

When our grievance was heard, it lasted for four hours, which is the longest grievance in the history of this grievance board. The grievance board was shocked with the bigoted statements and bullying that Stinson allowed Evelyn to administer to other inmates who entered the library. Stinson's defense was that he had tried to stop Evelyn but there was no controlling her. His whining only added to the contempt that the grievance board held for him. He was suspended for five days without pay and placed on probation.

He had even less control over Evelyn when he returned. As no disciplinary action had been taken against her resulting from the grievance, she felt she was infallible and continued her verbal bullying with even greater force.

Lucy and I agreed that we didn't need to work in such a negative environment and put in for job changes. I went to the commissary and Lucy went to work as a teacher's aide.

I filed a petition in the federal courts concerning job discrimination, and the federal courts ruled that 'no inmate was to be treated in a manner that was special or that would lead them to believe that they were superior to their peers.' Stinson was dismissed from his job for failing to control an inmate. Again, no action was taken against Evelyn.

Lucy finally agreed to move into my room. Several staff members later told me that the warden had discussed our relationship with them. They had all been in agreement with her that Lucy was a calming influence on me. However, they did add that they felt that I was very possessive of Lucy and would not hesitate to resort to violence if I felt she was being threatened. They also noted that despite her lady-like manner, Lucy was the dominate personality and would never approve of any violence on my part. They were all in agreement that it was a healthy relationship.

They were right in their evaluation of our relationship. I think when Lucy moved into my room, I was the happiest that I have ever been in my life. We would laugh over silly things on television or something someone had said to one of us during the day.

I enjoyed the homey chores of preparing us meals. Lucy would watch me with amusement while I fussed over the soup, tasting it to make sure it had the right amount of salt and pepper, or that it had cooked the right amount of time. Then I would wipe the spoon on my pants leg like an old man. Lucy would roll with laughter. Another time I was spreading the cheese on saltines. Lucy liked the salt on the cracker to be on the outside. I was deep into my chore, unaware that she was watching me. I would examine each cracker to ensure that I was spreading the cheese on the right side. I turned a cracker over several times in search of the salty side. Finally I solved the dilemma by putting it to the tip of my tongue to taste the salt. Lucy burst out with gales of laughter. "That's okay," she said, "just put the cheese on either side. It's not that important that the salt is on the outside."

Lucy believed in using her time wisely. She was always studying and encouraged me to study. If I balked at studying she would refuse to watch television with me over the weekend. There were many times I balked at her strict expectations of me. I would fly in a rage and throw my books and papers about the room. She would lie quietly across her bed until my anger had died and then I would resume my studies. We both completed three paralegal courses and I completed an electronic course.

Lucy was amazed at how quickly I learned the lessons—even pointing out errors in the text book. With the classes I took, my self-esteem soared. I realized the education I had missed out on and absorbed knowledge like a sponge drawing water.

Ms. Connie Seabrooks, the officer who had saved my life years before, had completed her education and was now the GED instructor and assistant principal of the school. She was a beautiful woman—both inside and out, and had remained my friend. She helped me to enroll in night college courses. I took an algebra class that I could use with my electronics course. Because of my interest in Vincent Van Gogh, I also took a course in art appreciation.

Officer Deak who had shown me compassion when I was in the dry cell and was being fed without the benefit of eating utensils, arranged for me to sing with a band that she was a member of when they visited the women's prison. I had written a song for my mother and Ms. Lynn Wilson—the librarian who took Stinson's place—helped me write the music to the song. I was proud of the accomplishment and the praise I received. Encouraged, I took piano lessons so that I would be able to write my own music.

There were still times when anger would fill me with hate and I wanted to strike out at the world, but Lucy seemed to sense these moods and head them off. She said she could see it in my eyes— they were cold and evil. She called them 'killer eyes.' She didn't condone the anger or resentment I felt for the past.

"The bitterness only destroys you," she would explain. "No one in the past cares if you hate them or not, so why destroy yourself by hating. Go on with your life and forget the past."

Soon it was hard to hate. If I tried to remember the mistreatment that I had been subjected to it was only vague memory.

Radeker—who had changed her name to Hoskins after her divorce—was soon to come under the close scrutiny of the media. One of the young inmates had gotten pregnant by an officer. The administrative staff were strongly encouraging the inmate to have an abortion. The news media caused a national scandal which resulted in an official investigation. Inmates were interviewed on television talk shows. Ten officers were fired as a result of the investigation.

Hoskins's coldness was brought to the public's attention again when an inmate was allowed to die in her dorm after crying for medical attention. The inmate lost control of all her bodily functions and the staff still insisted she was not in need of emergency treatment and refused to transport her to the hospital.

An investigation revealed that many medical staff members were refusing to administer needed medication to inmates and logging it as administered. One of the nurses who had participated in this fraud chose suicide over public prosecution and was found in her car overdosed on medication she had stolen from the institution.

Lucy believed that Hoskins was unaware of the cruelty that her staff members administered, and was guilty only of putting too much trust in the people who worked under her. In any event, Hoskins was moved to another institution. Penny Bernhardt took over. Staff and inmates alike noted the change in the morale.

I was among one of the first people who Ms. Bernhardt met when she arrived. She hugged my neck and congratulated me for my being in population.

"I've heard some very good reports concerning you, Lee," she praised.

"Thank you, I think I have come a long way since I first arrived."

"I have certainly heard about a different Lee than the one I knew in the seventies. Keep it up."

EPILOGUE

"Well, that about does it," the counselor announced. "I think we have everything we need. You have accomplished a lot in the last three years. Your behavior has progressed—I think the parole board will agree that you have really put forth an effort. Good luck to you, Lee."

"Thank you," I answered, and rose to leave the counselor's office.

I received her words with mixed feelings. I knew I could make it on the outside this time. I felt stronger emotionally. I also knew the importance of counseling and support groups. As I walked to the room Lucy and I shared, I thought of the nightmare of the last thirty years. It was a big price to pay for running off with a man's wife. I looked at the scars on my arms as I opened the door to our room. Yes, it was a big price to pay. I also knew that I have been happier in the past three years than I had been my whole life.

The clean, sweet smell of powders filled my nostrils as I entered the room. Lucy wasn't home from work yet, but her presence was everywhere. The room was decorated with matching pink bedspreads and a pink and green, floral hook-rug. Hand-crocheted doilies decorated the desk and dresser. Heart-shaped pillows of rose-colored satin and lace were tossed on the beds.

I sat on the edge of my bed and remembered when we first were told she was moving in. I had bunk beds and a metal locker—that was all. It was all I needed.

"Yick, it looks like a boy's locker room," Lucy teased.

Inmates were not allowed to move furniture from room to room but the guards on duty discreetly looked the other way while I not only moved furniture from another room, but from another hall, across the lobby and from another dorm across the yard. I exchanged the metal bunks for twin beds with wooden head-boards. I traded commissary for a matching dresser, hutch, night-stand and desk. I also added a wrought iron bookrack and match-ing towel rack, and a small, octagonal table. I covered the table with pink and white floral contact paper. Then I helped her move into my room. She laughed merrily when she saw what I had accom-plished.

"God, I can't believe you did all this. It looks great," she said as she walked around the room in amazement. "I can't believe this is the same room. Why didn't you do this a long time ago instead of the old junk you had?"

"I didn't have any reason to make it homey. It was just an ordi-nary prison room. It is home now."

I enjoyed nesting. Lucy said I didn't quite have the knack for it. She teased me because I would go about straightening rugs and smoothing wrinkles in the bedspread, then proceed to take a fan or radio apart on the bed, leaving an oily spot in the middle of the spread. She'd just laugh and shake her head. She said I had the per-sonalities of a child, an old man, and a bitchy old woman. The child and the old man were her friends, but the bitchy old woman always instigated arguments—short-lived arguments. Whenever we did disagree, Lucy insisted that I tell her why she was upset. She never wanted to risk my misunderstanding her anger, and the misunderstanding festering, and becoming something other than normal anger.

"Anger is an emotion, just like love, hate, happiness and sor-row, but it has to be handled with care or it will erupt someday without control—like a volcano. You need to be able to control it," she told me one day when we had just had a small spat.

Lucy was emotionally strong but I realized she had ostracized herself from the outside world. Her in-laws felt that her husband died in disgrace because of her charges, and had petitioned the courts to deny her parental rights. She had chosen to deny herself any other contact. I knew how hard it was to do your time alone. I also knew she wasn't as strong as she pretended. I knew of the crumpled tissues and the rosary she hid under her pillow, after cry-ing herself to sleep when she thought I was sound asleep.

172

I was thrilled to be going home after thirty years of incarceration, but it was breaking my heart to leave Lucy. I relived the nightmares of my fears from the parole eight years before.

The next few weeks were a time of emotional test for me. Two weeks before meeting the parole board, Captain Nixon escorted me to his office from my work area. Terror rose in me with each step. My heart felt as if it were being squeezed by a giant vise. I couldn't think of anything that I might have done to require escort, but from my past experiences, I feared it meant lock down. That was not the case, as I soon found out.

"Come in and sit down, Lee," Nixon said as I entered his office, but I did not sit. "Lee, the Warden has ordered me to tell you to shave your chin whiskers."

I wailed, "Why?"

"Because it is against policy." He stated with a pompous air.

After all these years, I knew policy! "I believe the policy states that women are not to cultivate facial hair. I have not cultivated this hair. I have had it since my early twenties. If I shave it, it will only grow back thicker and coarser. That is cultivating it."

"I'm just telling you what the Warden said."

I remembered Lucy telling me she didn't think Hoskins was aware of the rules that the officers enforced, and I sensed this was probably the case now. I also knew that Ms. Bernhardt would not allow an order that she hadn't authorized.

"Well, that seems pretty strange. The Warden has known me for over twenty years and never mentioned it before. I also believe she has been off sick all this week. When did she tell you this?" I challenged.

"Uh...I had a memo in my box," Nixon stammered.

"Could I see the memo?" Acutely aware that there probably wasn't one.

"I don't know where it is but I'm giving you a direct order to shave." He stated firmly.

I glared at him silently for a few seconds before I rose to go to my room and shave.

When the warden returned, I sent a message concerning what happened while she was off. She immediately called me to her office and apologized for any embarrassment Nixon caused me. I accepted, but also filed a petition in court against Nixon for his harassment.

The day the petition was filed, news of it was on the front page of *The Nashville Banner* and *The Tennessean*, the two largest state papers. Two television stations played a song from the fifties, *Shaving Cream*. They dedicated it to me. Staff and inmates ragged Nixon for days. He was a laughing stock.

The old Lee would have resorted to violence. I was proud of myself for the control I had exercised in the situation.

I met the parole board armed with a stack of certificates and an analysis of my violent history, noting the changes in my behavior and attitude since I had passed child-bearing age. I also noted, from what I read on the side effects of the medication I had been forced to take, that the mass amount of Thorazine had performed a sort of chemical lobotomy. Instead of calming me as the medication intended, it drove me insane and intensified my violent behavior.

The parole officer agreed with my analysis and recommended parole. Of course I still had to wait until the decision was granted from downtown—which meant Traughber would have to agree.

Thirty days later, I got the results on the parole hearing. Traughber denied my parole. I also noted that Ron Bishop was the other parole officer who signed the denial. Bishop was the warden of security who had tried to shoot me through the electrical socket when I had taken Officer Gore hostage. I felt that both men had a pretty negative attitude towards me.

I was ashamed to say I was not as disappointed as I should have been. How could you be disappointed in being allowed to stay with the one person who made you happy? I knew someday I would be allowed to go home. I had already been incarcerated longer than any woman in the history of Tennessee. Until that time I would be happy where I was. I would continue my education, maybe earn a degree before my release. Even in prison you could make your life worthwhile.

My petitions in the federal courts were precedent-setting cases which helped all incarcerated women. No longer could medication be forced on inmates. Inmates could not be held in solitary confinement without disciplinary reasons. My petitions to the court against Stinson concerning job discrimination and against Nixon forcing me to shave, caused changes in institutional policies.

I could look at these accomplishments and compare them with the scars on my arms. I guess they balanced the scales.

AFTERWORD

Well after the process of preparing Lee's story for publication had begun, Idella decided to submit her autobiography. Realizing that their fear of being separated had led to self-censorship in the writing of Lee's book, Idella decided to be more open and explicit in her story.

In the following letter, Idella describes the consequences of that decision.

Things here are really a mess. The manuscript I wanted to send you triggered the events.

Lee and I had discussed submitting my story with more emphasis on our relationship. We realized if it was accepted that it would be eighteen months or so before it was published so the chances of effecting us would be very slight. We both agreed it would be safe to go ahead and write what we really felt towards each other. We finished the final chapters and got it ready to mail. The woman in the mailroom always says something about the 'famous writer' and other snide remarks meant to embarrass me so Lee went to mail it. The woman insisted that Lee open it up to make certain that it wasn't state property, even though it was addressed to a publisher and the size of a manuscript. Lee opened it up, but became nervous. The woman noticed this and said that she thought she had better take the manuscript and review it to make sure it was Lee's. Lee told her that we were co-authors but the woman was insistent. Then Lee panicked because she was afraid that the last chapter would cause our separation, and so grabbing the manuscript, she tore it up. Her action caused an officer to call Internal Affairs. When the officers finally determined that they had no control over the content of the manuscript they returned the scraps to Lee—unread.

When she returned to the room she told me what had happened but assured me she had retrieved the manuscript and had disposed of all the pieces. I went crazy. It was my only copy of the manuscript and she had thrown it away. I had never been so angry with her. I asked to be put in voluntary segregation until I had calmed down. The dorm officer was more concerned with the content of the manuscript than my emotional state. She kept questioning me about the manuscript which added to my anxiety. Usually I am very quiet and reserved so my being upset made her more curious. After about two hours of her interrogation and my crying, it dawned on me I could get the pages out of the trash, tape them back together and retype. When the officer saw me going through the garbage cans, she got really agitated. She snatched the manuscript out of my hands and slugged me. I fell into another officer who was coming over to see what was happening. We both hit the floor and his body alarm went off. About eight officers were on top of me then. I was knocked out for a few seconds. They handcuffed me and dragged me to maximum. There I was thrown on a plastic mattress and stripped searched. I kept fading in and out of consciousness. I couldn't see for two hours, and my eyes didn't focus for several days after. One of my ears bled on the inside, and a filling in one of my teeth was knocked out.

The officer wrote me up for assault, threatening an officer, disrespect, failing to obey a direct order, creating a disturbance and conspiracy. Of course it's her word against mine and I'm the inmate. I was found guilty at the discipline board—the chairman was one of the officers who attacked me. I received thirty days in maximum security and ten days probation.

Lee was very concerned about me. I had given her a tiny recorder for Christmas a few years ago to record conversations of officers for her own protection, and so she got out her tape recorder. She recorded eight tapes of conversations with staff describing how the officer who wrote me up has a habit of slugging inmates, taking bribes and other unprofessional as well as illegal action, and that she has been warned about it many times.

She made three sets of tapes and sent one copy each to my attorney, the newspaper and the warden, and kept the original set. When the staff realized that she had recorded these conversations they became hostile, and really began to hassle her.

When I came out of maximum, the authorities put me into another dorm. They wouldn't let us room together, nor let her move to the same dorm. It has really broken her heart, and is tearing me up to see her so upset.

I talked with the warden, and she said that Lee needed to become more independent, that Lee depended on me too much. They were separating us for our own good. She felt it was too much of a burden for me always having to worry about Lee. I talked with her quite a while; I think she wanted to give in but she still had to back her staff. She said it wouldn't be but for a few months until everyone calmed down. I thought that Lee had regressed over the last month and wondered how she could handle a few more. She cut her hair very short—a sign to me that she was experiencing some self-loathing. I think she felt the whole incident was her fault.

Fortunately, our separation ended, but I continue to worry about us being separated again at any time. Our home, our moments of privacy remain uncertain, something to take day by day. Both Lee and I speculate that we were allowed to be together again because the authorities hoped she would erase all the tapes of testimony against the officers. Lee says that in her thirty years of incarceration, of being maced, handcuffed, shackled, beaten, kicked and locked in isolation for months, no punishment bothered her as much as the pain caused by our separation. And yet she refuses to let the fear of separation intimidate her into erasing the tapes.

When I look at Lee, her silver, curly hair, the dark half-Indian features, I find the combination attractive and exciting. Six years ago I would never have believed I was capable of loving another woman as much as I love Lee. I would have laughed had anyone suggested I would have a lesbian relationship. It is frightening to know that someone who loves you so much would go through such pain for you. I know in my heart she would even take a bullet for me if the situation called for it.

Our moments of privacy can only happen infrequently when we cover the wicket in the door to our cell with a towel. We have as long to touch, to be intimate as it takes for a passing guard to notice and order the towel to be taken down again.

Some day we will be able to sleep in each other's arms all

night. For now one of us must get up, remove the towel from the door and go to sleep in the other bed. Separated by inches, we are at least in the same cell. We are one no matter how close or distant the separation; we are there for each other.

Idella Serna on right, with Lee Dortch

Idella Serna has been self employed for the past twenty years as a small business tax-consultant as well as raising her half sister and two sons. She is currently serving a life sentence in the Tennessee Prison for Women, however the change in her environment has not slowed her down any. She stays busy tutoring other inmates, helping them understand the use of computers, helping them with legal research as well as working on her own degree in Business Administration. She is also writing an autobiograpy.